The Eighth Lively Art

THE
EIGHTH
LIVELY
ART

CONVERSATIONS WITH PAINTERS, POETS,

MUSICIANS, & THE WICKED WITCH OF THE WEST

WESLEY WEHR

UNIVERSITY OF WASHINGTON PRESS

SEATTLE & LONDON

Library of Congress Cataloging-in-Publication Data

Wehr, Wesley, 1929–
The eighth lively art : conversations with painters, poets,
musicians & the wicked witch of the west / Wesley Wehr.
p. cm.
Includes index.
ISBN 0-295-97956-9 (alk. paper)
1. Arts, Modern—20th century—Northwest, Pacific,
2. Artists—Northwest, Pacific. 3. Wehr, Wesley, 1929—
Friends and associates. I. Title
NX509.A1 W44 2000
700'.9795—dc21   00-021017

For
Ned Rorem
Robert B. Heilman
Gary Lundell

Contents

Acknowledgments

FOR INVALUABLE SUGGESTIONS and encouragement, I especially thank Guy Anderson, Helen Ballard, Kosme de Barañano, Dorothee Bowie, Peter Brazeau, Ree Brown, Giovanni Costigan, Henry Carlile, Rod Crawford, William Cumming, Paul Dahlquist, Lucienne Bloch Dimitroff, Don Ellegood, Gary Fountain, Brent Goeres, Gordon Grant, Morris Graves, Maxine Cushing Gray, Donald Grayson, Karen Hanson, Marshall Hatch, Rob Hause, Robert B. Heilman, Margaret Hodge, Randy James, Ray Kass, Solomon Katz, Martha Kingsbury, Leonard and Nancy Langer, Jo Lewis, Susan Libonati-Barnes, Gary A. Lundell, Beatrice Roethke Lushington, Francis McCue, Loren MacIver, Sandra McPherson, Joseph Newland, Elizabeth Patterson, Mary Randlett, Mark Ritter, Ned Rorem, Jean Russell, Oliver Sacks, Mimi Schorr, Francine

Seders, Mary O'Hara Selig, Leroy Soper, Jay Steensma, Herbert Steiner, Dale Stenning, Judi Sterling, Jan Thompson, John Uitti, Deryl Walls, Gretchen Van Meter, Elizabeth Bailey Willis, Karyl Winn, and De Wayne Young.

For their kind help and wise expertise, I am grateful to the staff of Manuscripts, Special Collections, University Archives Division, University of Washington Libraries.

Lastly, these acknowledgments would not be complete without my adding a few words of deep appreciation to one of the shining spirits of our time, Oliver Sacks, in gratitude for his friendship and encouragement.

Earlier versions of some of the essays in this book have appeared in the following publications: "Imogen Cunningham in San Francisco," "Ernest Bloch at Agate Beach," "Mark Tobey Conversations" (in ten parts), "Pehr Hallsten and Mark Tobey," in *Northwest Arts* during 1976–80, Maxine Cushing Grey, editor; "Elizabeth Bishop: Conversations & Class Notes," in *The Antioch Review* (Summer 1981); "Elizabeth Bishop and Susanne K. Langer: A Conversation," in *The Harvard Review*, Stratis Haviaris, editor (Winter 1993); "Out of Nature: Natural History in Mark Tobey's Art," *Reina Sofia National Museum*, Madrid (1997); "Theodore Roethke in the Classroom," in *The Seattle Review* (Summer 1998). Portions of "Elizabeth Bishop in Seattle" have been quoted in Gary Fountain and Peter Brazeau, *Remembering Elizabeth Bishop: An Oral History*, University of Massachusetts Press (1994).

The Eighth Lively Art

A Totemic
Introduction

O NCE LONG AGO, in a then-remote region called the Pacific Northwest, there was a lovely, heavily forested, sparsely populated wilderness at the edge of the Pacific Ocean. It could rain relentlessly there. Weeks, if not months, could pass without any of us in Seattle, the largest city in this territory, being able to catch even a glimpse of fog-enveloped Mount Rainier some eighty miles to the southeast. The damp, rainy winters often seemed interminable. But this, we philosophically told ourselves, was good for the towering cedar, fir, and hemlock trees, and for the blackberries, huckleberries, and rhododendrons that grew profusely in the forests surrounding our coastal cities and towns. There were still vestiges of ancient totem poles on some of the islands far to the north. Our beaches glistened with moonstone agates and brightly colored jasper, especially after the winter storms. The many native species of clams, oysters, salmon, crab, and halibut were bountiful, seemingly inexhaustible.

There were many local painters, poets, and musicians, too. But not, of course, nearly so many as there are now. During the rainy months, they frequently huddled together in steamy coffee shops on Seattle's University Way or in the downtown Public Market, the painters exchanging their drawings with fellow painters, the poets dedicating their poems to fellow poets. And there were those who drank (and drank) beer together, especially at the Blue Moon Tavern in the University District. But that's another story, and I'm not the one to tell that story.

Those were good years, the 1950s and early 1960s, although they didn't always seem so at the time. They were good partly because most of the artists were usually so broke. In our mutual poverty there flourished our sense of community. The artists didn't compete so aggressively then for money because, with the exception of generous souls such as art patron Richard E. Fuller, founder and director of the Seattle Art Museum, and a few other patrons and collectors, there wasn't much money around. There were scarcely any foundation grants, and not much public art. Most of the artists here held to the idea that a "career" was something people had in Hollywood.

Perhaps some of the artists during those years, myself included, suffered from a regional mass delusion. We talked a lot about destinies and artistic callings. We read books about Zen. We read Coomaraswamy's *Nature and the Transformation of Art*, Meister Eckhart's *Sermons*, and Thoreau's *Walden*. The Asian contemplative philosophies permeated the artistic scene in the Pacific Northwest. There was so little immediate success to vie for that we local artists obviously had to take the long view of things.

Some of the artists, such as Mark Tobey, even tried their hand at meditation, but not very successfully. Meditation was not Tobey's cup of tea. He wrote in his private diary while he was staying in a Kyoto monastery in 1934, "The gong has just sounded for meditation. I don't want to go, but I can't think of another excuse." It was the Japanese aesthetic that inspired Tobey. Japanese American artist George Tsutakawa once explained to me, "Tobey introduced me to the beauty of Japanese art. I was so busy learning about Western art that I didn't realize what a great tradition I had come from. Tobey understood and appreciated the greatness of the Japanese aesthetic and introduced us Japanese Americans here to it." In a documentary film on Tsutakawa's life, he added, "You know — when I was trying to paint like Braque, Picasso, Matisse — Tobey said, 'What are you doing? Why don't you look back and see what your ancestors did?'"

Tobey did take Zen very seriously — to a point. He told his friends they should never claim he had "achieved enlightenment," or any such thing. Shortly before he died, Tobey told his friend Mark Ritter, "I tried as best I could to understand Zen. It would be pretentious for me to claim I ever had a grasp of it, let alone achieved enlightenment." Once, when Tobey had finished reading a new book by Zen writer Nancy Wilson Ross, he exclaimed, "Oh, there goes Nancy again! She thinks the world can be saved by a cup of tea!"

Some of the earlier artists — Mark Tobey, Morris Graves, Guy Anderson, and Kenneth Callahan, in particular — had discovered that "mysticism" and geographical isolation could go hand-in-hand with widespread recognition, and that indeed it held for New Yorkers and other such outsiders a certain romantic and exotic cachet. *Life* magazine's 1953 feature article on these four artists was entitled "Mystic Painters of the Northwest." This article brought the art world's attention, both locally and nationally, to the work of these four painters as well as to the pristine natural beauty of the Pacific Northwest. Morris Graves's seclusiveness was well publicized, as were his social and his antisocial unpredictability. Guy Anderson put it best: "One day Morris discovered a socially acceptable way of slapping people in the face and being thanked for it by them. It's called 'The Zen Slap!' The Zen masters slapped their disciples to wake them up, to snap them out of it, when they thought it was necessary."

Nevertheless, many of the local artists did indeed take to heart the tenets of Zen and Chinese philosophy. This was especially true during the 1960s of the group of young painters and poets who lived at Fish Town, on the Skagit River, just south of La Conner.

THE DAY THE SEATTLE WORLD'S FAIR opened in 1962 marked a turning point. The scene, for better or for worse, has never been quite the same. Seattle on that day stopped being a big town and became a small city in the nationwide grand scheme of things. The artists started to smell money in the air, and for some of them it was much sweeter than the smell of cedar bark or Wenatchee Valley apples. There was no turning back. Cultural missionaries began to arrive in droves from New York. Seattle became something akin to Joseph Conrad's Outpost of Progress. It was still "out of it," but not quite. The times were rapidly changing. There was still hope, according to the more progressively minded members of the art community, for a less provincial, more cosmopolitan and "relevant" cultural scene in the Pacific Northwest—one less rooted in Asian and European art of the past.

DURING THE 1960S, I first began to read James Boswell's recorded conversations with Dr. Samuel Johnson. Next I discovered *Table Talk*, in which William Hazlitt had set down pithy and revelatory exchanges between many of the leading poets and writers in early nineteenth-century England. He had caught the flavor and gusto of how such writers as Wordsworth, Coleridge, Southey, and Lamb conversed in an everyday way. These accounts were fascinating for their unguarded immediacy—so unlike formal interviews.

Boswell and Hazlitt caught me up short. There would be little awareness in the future of how such Northwest painters as Mark Tobey, Pehr Hallsten, Guy Anderson, Morris Graves, and Helmi Juvonen once talked "off the record" during the 1950s and 1960s. And the same held true for a wealth of other voices—art dealer Zoe Dusanne—poets Theodore Roethke, Richard Selig, Elizabeth Bishop, and Léonie Adams—Miss Bishop having dinner with philosopher Susanne K. Langer— pianist Berthe Poncy Jacobson—composer Ernest Bloch talking to two young music students one winter afternoon on the Oregon coast—photographer Imogen Cunningham, nearly ninety and in top form—actor Margaret Hamilton advising an aspiring young actor. How did each of these remarkable individuals converse informally? My concern was with

dialogue, with catching somehow the flavor of their sponta-
neous words.

And so, the rudiments of this book fell into place. I first
began to take notes on my conversations with friends during
a 1956 visit with Susanne K. Langer in Old Lyme, Connecticut. One evening she had said several things that I especially
wanted to remember. Later that night, in her upstairs guest
room, I wrote them down. The following year I found myself
similarly motivated by an evening of good talk when artist
Mark Tobey was in particularly fine form. I was soon routinely writing down not only what Tobey said to me but also
my conversations with other artists, musicians, and writers.
Sometimes I wrote these comments in my diaries. Other times
I recorded them in letters to close friends, or on stray scraps of
paper which I would later transcribe. Not being confident
that I had always caught the gist or the exact words of these
conversations, I made every effort later to run them past various close friends of the people whose words I had recorded.
I would get a quick smile of recognition, or a "That's it!" — and
I knew I was on the right track.

On several occasions, I parroted back to Mark Tobey a
year or so later what he had said earlier to me, not telling him
that I was quoting him.

"That sounds pretty sensible. Who told you that?"

"You did! Last year, at this very table," I answered.

Another time, after I had again quoted him anonymously,
he snapped, "What jackass ever told you a thing like that?"

I knew better than to answer, "You did, a year ago!"

IN 1949, MARY RANDLETT PHOTOGRAPHED Mark
Tobey, Morris Graves, and their New York dealer Marion

Willard in Graves's back yard at Woodway Park, near Edmonds, Washington. By the mid-sixties, Mary had swung into
full action, photographing many of the region's painters, poets, and writers. Her energy and thoroughness were prodi-
gious — and timely. During the fifties and sixties there was an
ongoing discussion hereabouts as to the existence, real or
imaginary, of the so-called Northwest School of regional
painting and writing. Poet Carolyn Kizer finally sized up the
situation, declaring: "I don't know if there's a Northwest
School, but I do know that by the time Mary and her camera
have finished photographing all of us, there certainly will be.
Mary will have seen to it!" Carolyn referred to Mary as "our
court photographer."

THIS BOOK is by no means a comprehensive account of all
the painters, writers, and musicians who set the pace and
tone for the various arts in the Pacific Northwest during the
1950s and 1960s. It is instead a reflection of my own particular friendships with a handful of those creative figures during
a critical period in the artistic history of this region. Along
with some ruminations on the fact that, for artists themselves
in their lives and work, the arts *are* interrelated, it consists of
conversations and personal exchanges with a dozen or so of
the individuals who best defined and exemplified the arts,
and who lived for a time in the Northwest. I was fortunate
to know many of them as close friends. A chance remark
by one of them would sometimes turn out to be the only surviving record of an important glimpse into an artist's private
thoughts and feelings, the wellspring of artistic motivation. It
was often this casual, unguarded remark that proved to be the
most revealing.

What do these strongly individual, creative people have in common? They certainly share an exceptional independence of spirit, a high degree of stubbornness, and a determination to go one's own way, whether it leads to eventual recognition or not. Whatever it is that distinguishes them, decade after decade these same qualities continue to reappear in many forms among the painters, poets, and musicians in the Pacific Northwest. I call their voices and stories "totemic" because the people I record and write about in this book, although they can often seem so very dissimilar, do share complex kinships — creative relationships that are subtle at times, and hard to pinpoint, but distinctive kinships all the same in their infinite ways of being singularly creative.

SOME PAINTERS &
A PHOTOGRAPHER

Conversations with Mark Tobey

M Y INTRODUCTION to Mark Tobey took place under unusual circumstances. During the summer of 1949, I unexpectedly became his tutor in music composition. Tobey was nearly sixty years old and I was nineteen. Besides being a painter, Tobey was a gifted amateur composer. I was a music composition major at the University of Washington. We both studied privately with the composer Lockrem Johnson. When Lockrem was away from Seattle that summer, studying music composition with the great French composer Olivier Messaien, Tobey's close friend, pianist Berthe Poncy Jacobson, suggested that I might pinch-hit for Lockrem as a temporary tutor for Tobey. To me the prospect seemed a bit overwhelming.

Mrs. Jacobson took me to Tobey's house on Brooklyn Avenue in the University District. He was disarmingly cordial.

He promptly brought me a cup of very good coffee and a bit of Danish pastry and started to show me his latest paintings. Mrs. Jacobson smiled, clearly pleased with how quickly Tobey had put me at ease.

The lessons were to be weekly. Soon Tobey suggested I should feel free to visit him more often, or even come to his studio. "If I'm too busy to see anyone, I'll tell you so," he said. "Otherwise, I'd enjoy visits from you. We can talk about music. I talk enough about painting as it is. If you talk about a painting too much while you're working on it — or show it to people before it's finished — as far as your subconscious is concerned that painting is *finished!*"

SOME YEARS LATER, over dinner one evening in 1957, Tobey said to painter Arthur Hall Smith and me, "Now this is important. You will need to remember this." He then quoted a remark from Leonardo Da Vinci: "All nature bends before the will of man." I promptly wrote down this remark and soon began noting other things Tobey said to me. He talked about so many things — about art, music, life — that I was usually at sea to figure out just what I should record. So I simply wrote down everything: the profound remarks, the trivial tirades, all of it! I was secretive about these notes, afraid that he wouldn't talk so freely if he suspected I had become some sort of self-appointed Boswell.

At times my behavior must really have puzzled him. We might be sitting at his dinner table, or having coffee at Manning's coffee shop on University Way, when Tobey would say something especially arresting, something I needed to remember. But there were too many words! Too many

*In the garden at Morris Graves's home in Woodway Park at Edmonds,
Washington, August 1949. Left to right: art dealer Marion Willard,
Morris Graves, Mark Tobey, and Graves's dog, Edith
(Photograph by Mary Randlett)*

ideas! My memory simply couldn't keep up with it. Finally, in desperation, I would excuse myself from the table and make a beeline for the nearest bathroom to jot down what he had just said. Wherever we met — in Seattle, San Francisco, New York — we sat in coffee shops and consumed oceans of coffee. I'm sure Tobey began to wonder if I didn't have just about the smallest and weakest bladder in the world.

The secrecy especially bothered me. Finally, one day in Seattle in 1960, I confessed to him that I had been taking notes. He was silent for a moment, and then said, "One of my students used to take notes on our talks. When I read them I could have puked. I saw an awful lot of her in what she had written down, and very little of myself. It's all right with me that you're taking notes on our conversations, but maybe you'd better let me read through them sometime. Who knows? You might just become some sort of biographer of mine some day. I guess I could do worse than that! But if you ever do, please don't let me sound too pompous and cocksure."

What follows here are some of Tobey's comments, quoted from various conversations, along with my own recollections. I wrote down what he said as soon as I could, either in private diaries or on scrawled scraps of paper. Later I transcribed them into notebooks. The earlier notes can seem a bit like "The Sayings of," but I was eager to listen and learn — and Tobey was glad to teach.

"WHEN I WAS A YOUNG PAINTER, there were quite a few painters around me who had every bit as much talent as I did — and some of them had a lot more. But there was one thing I had they didn't have. Sheer Yankee cussed stubbornness! I took my work pretty seriously, but I didn't take *myself* all that seriously."

"I WAS NEVER VERY CLOSE to my family — my mother as much as any of them. My brother was ten years older than I was. My father was the spit 'n' image of Mark Twain, mustache and all. He was a carpenter and quite artistic, considering his background. Now and then he would sit down and draw a two-storey house, and it would really be pretty good. Ben Hecht's book on that whole period in Chicago is the one to read. He did it very well. But that time is gone forever now, and it won't come back. The first Tobey was in America in 1610.

"I can remember so many beautiful summers that came and went. And where was I? In the studio, working, working. Maybe I should have taken off more time to enjoy life, but it's too late to think about that now. No, I'm certainly not a genius, and I never was one. I simply wanted to paint, and I had to work very hard at it. I'm not one of those people who can learn quickly and easily. I have to learn things by a kind of osmosis."

MANY OF TOBEY'S SINGULAR REMARKS came from occasions when I brought him paintings of my own for comment. During the Christmas holiday of 1960, I bought some tempera paints and a box of wax crayons. I had no intention of becoming a painter, let alone any pretentions in that direction. The winter months were rainy and gloomy in the University District. My music composing was going badly, and I was burned out on reading books. I began to paint a few small landscapes and seascapes. They resembled the nature images one could imagine in "thunder egg" agates from Oregon and polished petrified wood from eastern Washington.

Several months later, when Tobey returned to Seattle from Europe, I asked him if he would look at a group of these little pictures. He suggested I leave some of my paintings at his house. He would spend some time with them and tell me what he thought of them later in the week. Five days later the proverbial "moment of truth" had come. Tobey had looked at the work. He was encouraging enough, but he was curious about my own seriousness:

"Do you want to become a painter? Do you realize how *many* painters there are? Why, there must be about a million of them in Paris alone. The way it is now, an artist has to be original. He can't just paint well; he has to have his own angle of vision. You don't have to be a 'major' painter — some of my own favorite painters are usually called 'minor.' But you do have to have something that is your own, something worthwhile and distinctive."

Did I want to be a painter? My answer surprised him a bit: "Mark, I just want to paint. If other people end up calling me a painter, that will be okay with me. I've realized lately that even if you tell me today that I have no talent for painting, and I have no future as 'a painter,' I'll probably just go ahead and paint anyway."

Tobey looked me in the eye, and burst into laughter: "You're an odd duck! So you would go ahead and paint anyway, even if I told you I thought you had no future? That's what I hoped you would say! By the way, how important is approbation to you? Not too important, I hope. If I have to, I know pretty well how to live modestly and get on with my work. I can enjoy a bit of luxury now and then—but I don't need to have it all the time."

SO MANY OF MY FRIENDS from student days were becoming concerned about "security." They were giving up any idea of being artists or poets. They talked more and more about money, about "well-paying jobs," and "careers." I went to visit Tobey and told him how upset I was by all of this.

"Security? You're asking *me* about security? Look at me—I'm almost seventy now and I don't even own any property. Very often I don't even know where my next money is going to come from. If you want to be a painter, don't put things off too much. The conditions will *never* be ideal! One way or another, I manage to get by—and I do keep painting!"

I RAN INTO TOBEY at Manning's coffee shop. I had just finished a new picture. He looked at it. The next day he commented on it: "That painting you showed me yesterday has beautiful color, very beautiful color. But you *made* that picture. I didn't see much real spirit in it. Frankly, I like your more clumsy things better. Now don't go and turn into one of those aesthetic object-machines. I have to be on guard against it all the time myself. You might read Robert Henri's little book, *The Art Spirit*. It's a very good one. Keep it around and read it now and then. You won't go astray with that book, I promise you!"

It annoyed Tobey that so many of the young painters he met seemed to know more about the local gallery scene than about the great masters of the past. He found many of the painters to be more preoccupied with local reputations and acceptance than with visiting great museums. He suggested that I go back to New York again. "There's a nice poetic quality in the Northwest, but what this area lacks is *sandpaper*— something more stimulating, even abrasive. Painters just don't develop unless they have some sandpaper. Why don't you go to New York for a while? That will shake you up!"

I ARRIVED ONE AFTERNOON AT MANNING'S coffee shop to find Tobey sitting in a booth next to the window. He waved me over. We began to talk. I said, "Mark, there's a painter I know here in the University District. I rather like him, he's pleasant enough. But I don't like his paintings at all. They seem empty and pointless."

"If I don't like someone's work," he answered, "I can't really like the person. Because what we create is what we really are. We wear so many social masks when we're with people. Goethe said, 'Look for the man in the work.' When I look at Picasso's work, I see Picasso the man—his thought, his energy, his restlessness. So much painting I see these days tells me absolutely nothing about the artist who painted it, nothing about what he loves, nothing about what he believes in. The world is becoming impersonal enough as it is, and now the cult of the impersonal appears all through painting."

Tobey's one and only application for a Guggenheim Fellowship had not met with any success when he was young. "I applied for a Guggenheim once. That was the first time and the last time I did that. When the results were in, a man I knew on the board took me out for lunch. He said to me, 'I'm sorry, Mark. We had better material this year.' It turned out that some guy who painted green nudes got it. They were awful paintings, but he was well connected. I've never heard a thing about him since."

By the early 1960s, Tobey was now a famous painter. That, however, didn't exempt him from being rejected by a local art jury: "Well, Papa Tobey himself just got rejected from the Northwest Annual yesterday. I put in one of my best sumi pictures—the seated woman. Sure it's nice to get into these shows, even when you know that the juror is a real jackass. Sometimes a few more of your pictures will sell because of the publicity, and one can always use the money. But if you start worrying about pleasing jurors, you're headed for turning into a real hack. Real paintings are usually ahead of their time, and only a few people can see and appreciate them at first. I've known a lot of professional prizewinners. They know exactly what the jury wants and they can dish it up to order. They could just as well design dresses or automobiles."

"IT'S GOING TO BE THE JOB of your generation to rescue art from all the jargon and intellectualism. In America we're victims of journalism. The way we throw the word *genius* around these days is really something! I would call Michelangelo, Beethoven, and Mozart geniuses.—The young artists' growth is being constantly interrupted by all the attention to prizes, early reputations, scholarships. Prizes are dynamite— especially for young artists. I read prize lists not to find out what is good but to watch how the winds blow this way and that. Be careful to whom you turn for approbation. It may sound arrogant, but I'm pretty fussy about which compliments have meaning for me now."

"YOU'VE GOT TO BE ABLE to let go of success as quickly as it comes to you. Don't be trapped by it. I've been in fashion and I've been out of fashion enough times already that

I've learned to keep a distance on both of them. I was a fashionable portrait painter in New York when I was young, and then I got tired of all of that. Stay away from all those people and their parties. People will devour you alive if you let them have half the chance. What's that old saying?—I can handle my enemies, but God save me from some of my friends!"

"DON'T BE TOO ANXIOUS to be a part of your times, to be 'with it,' as they say. Those times and fads change so fast, and so many artists get stuck in all the affectations of those passing-isms. Be interested in the entire history of art and not just in what happens to be going on at the moment."

"DON'T BE IN SUCH A RUSH to find yourself. Until I was about fifty they used to call me the sleeping child. I was interested in everything when I was young—poetry, music, dance. Of course, I'm still interested in many things, but there's so little now to inspire me from the outside. Life doesn't burn into me the way it used to. More and more I have to draw from myself and find the inspiration in myself. [Painter Lyonel] Feininger wrote me a while ago that there's no geographic retreat now. We don't have a Tahiti to go to like Gauguin, the way it was when we were young. The world has grown too small for that now. We have to find such a place, he said, within ourselves now."

"I HATE THIS UNIFORMITY that's spreading over the world. And the worst of it is that it consists of the most impersonal and plastic aspects of our time. We're tearing down so many old and beautiful things, and calling it Progress.

That isn't progress — it's an insane kind of busywork. So little is built now to last for very long. Things are thrown together, and then they fall apart. When we lose the pride and satisfaction of really trying to do things well, we're headed for serious trouble. Shortcuts be damned! I want nothing to do with that mentality."

"IT'S ALL RIGHT, Wes, that you're composing music and also painting pictures now; doing both of them will enrich you. But a time will come when one of these things will dominate your attention more than the other. Then you'll have to concentrate more on that one thing. You can't be an ear and an eye at the same time! But I can say this: whatever you are doing at the moment — whether it's writing music, painting some pictures, writing a poem — whatever it is, give it your full attention! Give it everything you've got!

"I think it's a good thing that you have all of these interests at this time in your life. It's that hobby of yours — what do you call it? Oh, yes — rockhounding. That interest of yours in agates and fossils is going to save your neck in the long run, I predict!"

WHEN I FIRST MET him, Tobey was feeling somewhat sorry for himself. He felt that he deserved more recognition than he was receiving, especially from the New York art critics. A few years later, however, he began to win many important prizes, both nationally and internationally. His attitude about fame and recognition changed. One day he said to me: "I wouldn't wish fame on my worst enemy. It's a headache — all the deadlines, the people wanting pictures all the time.

Don't get any notion that fame and success mean that more people finally understand your work. A lot of it's just lip service, and usually it only means that you've arrived in some social way that has very little to do with what you paint. Believe me, I get awfully tired of being *Mark Tobey*!

"My happiest times were on University Way—those long winters when I could work and work on a painting, think about it, work on it again. There were a few people who liked my work, who would buy it now and then, who kept me going. Not many artists survive being discovered. It makes them too self-conscious.

"Before I became one of these 'famous' painters, people used to be pretty direct with me about my work. They'd tell me right off when they didn't like something. Now so many people fawn over every little thing I paint until I start to wonder what's wrong with those people! When you get to be famous, you're lucky if you still have a few friends who will be honest with you and not just flatter you all the time. You've got to be more self-critical than ever, because your flatterers can't see past your reputation. Every time after I've had a big exhibition, it's like crawling out of my own grave to get started again. During the Louvre show, what I was really thinking to myself was: Can I paint another picture when this damned thing is over?—My favorite show was that retrospective at the Seattle Art Museum—with all those paintings owned and loaned by old friends of mine."

A YOUNG PAINTER asked me to introduce him to some Seattle dealers. He also asked if I would help him sell some of his paintings to collectors who were buying my own works. I mentioned this to Tobey.

"Don't help the young too much," he responded. "It will just weaken them and they'll only resent it. Pretty soon they'll start avoiding you. You can open a few doors for them and introduce them to a few people. But don't meddle with their initiative. Don't turn into an advice-factory. People have to find out things for themselves, in their own ways. What's good for you may not be good for them, and vice versa.

"What's so wrong with having problems, anyway? Problems are an important part of maturing—meeting them straight on, working them out. It's like the chick in the egg. It has to break through the eggshell on its own. That's how it gains its first strength. If you step in and break the shell for the chick, you end up with a puny little runt."

ONE AFTERNOON IN 1958 I came into Tobey's University District studio to find a large painting on the easel. It was a fairly typical work, well painted, but not all that exciting. It was the kind of painting that could sell quickly in New York. Tobey had just turned down some thousands of dollars for it. The dealer visiting his studio had explained that he would take it "as it is" since he had a plane to catch in a few hours. Tobey was upset by the dealer's assumption that, finished or not, the painting was for sale—if the price was right.

"He wanted to buy it on the spot, even though I told him repeatedly that I wasn't finished with it. Can you imagine! He told me it was just *fine* for him. He offered me a lot of money for it if I would let him have it just as it is. I couldn't do that. And I hope I never have to! I'd rather die in the poorhouse than start giving in to that sort of thing!"

He kept on pacing and fuming: "Sometimes I get so exasperated with these dealers when they ask me to send more things of a certain kind, more big pictures, more small pictures. I can't work that way. For some reason or another, my painting *Homage to Rameau* is popular right now. Maybe it has something to do with the title. And, as usual, a number of people want one just like it. Before that, they wanted more white-writing paintings. I can't paint to order that way. When I lose interest in something, it's over. I have to go on to something else. Now and then I may recapitulate something I've done, but it's just to try my hand at it again. You're a musician —you know the difference between recapitulating a theme and merely repeating yourself. Then you have to move on. As Edvard Munch said: 'Where you are now, I once was and am no longer.'

"But if you have a *good* dealer, try to stick with him. Some painters change galleries all the time. All that hopping around isn't good for the gallery. And make sure it's a dealer who respects what you're doing, a dealer you really like as a friend. Otherwise it's just a temporary business arrangement. A good dealer believes in you and slowly educates people to your work."

By now, he'd put his brushes away: "It's amazing how many bad paintings the modern masters have done. You see them all over Europe, pictures changing hands all the time because they're no good. From the look of it, you'd swear that some of our modern artists never destroyed or threw out *anything*. The fashions change; reputations come and go. The poor works by a famous painter are almost worthless later, when his fashion and reputation have cooled down. But there's usually some collector or museum who will always want the best works by an artist, even when he isn't as famous as he used to be. A great portrait by Gainsborough is always good, no matter how much the fashions change."

WHEN I ARRIVED at Tobey's studio another afternoon, he was working on a large painting. He hoped, he said, to be able to finish it in time to include it in his exhibition at the Venice Biennale. "This painting has *got* to be good. There will be all those [Mark] Rothko paintings in the next room at the Biennale. My things will be lost besides those large, beautiful things of his! Make yourself at home for a while."

"I'm surprised you don't seem to mind my being here while you're painting."

"The people I could do this with are few and far between, believe me."

Tobey continued to work. He was displeased with the way the painting was going: "Now I'm starting to get too acrobatic with this picture. Rothko would just have a few broad edges and then fuzz the edges. But if I understand what I'm trying to do here, it's something quite different." He paused, and stepped back several feet to study the painting. He decided to try something quite different. He quickly covered the surface of the painting with calligraphic strokes. In some areas it seemed to work quite well; in other areas it didn't work at all.

Tobey noticed a small form in the painting, a shape that annoyed him. "That looks like the man in the moon! Out it comes!" he said, quickly obliterating the offending form. "I'm just not pleased at all with this painting. I thought I was almost through with it, but now I see that I'm just starting. It's hard work. Maybe I'm trying to follow nature too closely. If I do this, it means I have to do that. All these little forms have to relate to each other without becoming merely busy. *That* little form has to come out now. How to accent without the accent detaching itself from the picture plane. You've got to be on your toes watching for that. It's always the same problem. Too much, too little. These things stick out like a sore thumb when I'm working."

Tobey started to move the painting about the studio, nearer the window, where the afternoon winter light was stronger. He stood close to the painting; he stepped back to look at it from a distance. "See, Wes, when I place the painting in less light, the details disappear and you see the severe bands again. *They* stand out too much. When the painting was in that different light across the room, the *details* stood out too much! Lord, it's got a dry surface! I have to keep figuring how the brush stroke will dry. Well, I've known all along that I'd have to relate this area of the painting to the rest of it. And here's *another* bad spot in it! I'll have to do something about that too! If you stand over here and look at it, it's a real rainbow of color. It keeps changing all the time when I move it into a different light. I keep finding more and more things wrong with it. I have to paint it in such a way that this picture will stand its ground in any kind of viewing light."

"Mark, do you have to include this painting in the Biennale? If you don't include it, will you have enough paintings?"

"I don't want to send it to Venice if it's going to look like a 'small' painting. When I stand off from it, it looks small. And now it starts to look large again at a different distance. Oh, I'm afraid I won't be able to do it. Maybe I should just paint all of this out." Tobey toned down the broad bands of color, and added more accents to the picture. "Pink is the damnedest color to paint over. It comes right through the white here. This is a devilish piece to work on. And now I'm getting careless with it."

After a long look at the painting, Tobey took a wet sponge and wiped out a good part of it. "I'm getting nowhere today. Let's go to Manning's for some coffee!"

AS WE WALKED DOWN UNIVERSITY WAY to Manning's coffee shop, a faint aroma of marijuana wafted from a doorway where several teenagers stood. Tobey also noticed them. "One certainly doesn't need to take drugs to have visions. If you're flat broke and haven't eaten for several days, you'll start seeing *plenty* of things! One time in Chicago, I hadn't had a square meal for days. When I came back to my hotel room, my landlady said I looked like a ghost. I had the feeling I could have walked right through the walls and not have bothered with the door. I used to sit in my hotel room there, and the wallpaper would start dancing. A man with a green hat in the street. Painters in white uniforms on a scaffolding. These things would almost knock me over. This is a sense which can be developed — this intensity in the way one sees things."

Tobey was still frustrated by the afternoon's unsuccessful painting session. "Some days I just can't seem to get down to work. I'll go to the studio. I'll work for hours and hours — and nothing happens. But an artist should spend at least several hours every day at his work, just to keep his hand in it. With all my technique, I should be able to make a little thing when I want to, but it isn't like that now. I daub at one thing, and then another — and nothing happens. Painting is work, work, work. A painter should be looking at things, feeding on everything, sketching things, jotting down ideas. Sometimes, of course, you'll be distracted by something else and start doing that for a while. I'll spend weeks composing little pieces for the piano, maybe writing something. But if you're really meant to be a painter, you won't stay away from it too long. You'll keep coming back to it."

TOBEY SETTLED IN BASEL, Switzerland, during the early 1960s. His companion, Pehr Hallsten, died in Basel in 1965. The next year Tobey's Seattle dealer and close friend Otto Seligman died in Seattle. Tobey had lost two of his closest friends. He returned to Seattle for brief visits during both 1966 and 1967. I wondered if he would have any more advice for me during those last visits to Seattle. I told him I had been doing very little painting.

"If you don't enjoy painting, why go on with it? I see so *many* works that have no energy whatsoever. They look as if the painter didn't care about *anything*. They turn the act of painting into just a bad habit," he responded.

I must have had an uneasy look on my face. My own painting wasn't going at all well. In fact, it was so spiritless that even I could see that I was in a dismal slump. Tobey noticed my wince and hastened to add, "Oh, I don't mean you, Wes. Please don't get me wrong. Your landscapes have a nice poetic quality. But I can't always tell how strong your artistic will is. I haven't especially liked some of the recent paintings you've shown me, not nearly as much as the first ones you showed me several years ago. Maybe you need to do something else for a while—maybe some rockhounding. Or go to the Oregon coast and collect some more agates."

TOBEY HAD ONCE ENCOUNTERED me standing on a University Way corner on a summer afternoon in 1958. He studied my glazed expression carefully, "The way you've been acting lately, you've got all the signs of being in love. Bouncing around with that idiotic grin on your face! Where were you last Friday? We had a lunch date, you know. I guess you forgot. Falling in love does do that sort of thing to one. All these infatuations of yours! Sometimes I can't keep track of even half of them. Well, I'm glad you're enjoying life. I know I've said things to you about how a painter has to work and work. And how one needs to be alone to get anything done. This other thing, being in love, is important too! But when you're in love, I hope it's with someone you *like*. It's an awful thing to be attached to someone you don't even like. I could tell you a few things about that! I think you're a little like me — you need someone quiet and steady. And if you do meet someone like that, what a difference it can make.

"You're at that time in your life now when you're going to be meeting many people, but only a few of them will finally be very important to you. Sometimes it will be the most unlikely people who will have a profound influence on you — opening you up to things, inspiring you, giving you enough steady friendship and stability that you can quiet down and get something done. I think that what you're looking for is a fellow student.

"But very few people remain students, I'm sorry to say. Oh, I don't mean in the school sense, of course. No, it's someone who keeps learning, growing, changing for a whole lifetime — a companion with whom you can explore the world. If you find such a person, you're very fortunate. Maybe it's a kind of gift from God. And if you don't, then you make your journey alone. I've had to make big decisions about my own life along the way. Quite frankly, I'll *never* really know if they were the best decisions—but having made those decisions I've had to abide by them. We never really know where our journeys will take us. It's like Christopher Columbus. We look for one thing and find something quite different. The important thing is that Columbus got into a ship and he set sail. And if you want to find something, you have to get into your own ship and set sail!

"You're shy, like me. These infatuations will get you out of yourself for a while, but don't become addicted to being 'happy.' Real happiness will take you by surprise when you least expect it. It probably won't last very long, because life is constant change, and there's a little sadness mixed in with everything we experience in life. My shyness has caused me some real problems. If I became fond of someone, I'd be too embarrassed to show it at first. When I finally did, I'd scare the daylights out of them with the suddenness and intensity of my feelings. They'd flee, and that would make me even more shy than ever.

"Did I ever tell you I was married once? It's quite a story. I knew this woman and we were getting on pretty well. She would say that we should get married, and I would work on my art, and she would stand by me through thick and thin. I wanted to get married. It all sounded pretty good. So we got married. The next thing I knew, we were sitting at the dinner table and she was carrying on about how I would have to give up my pretensions to being an artist, how I would have to give it all up and go out and find an honest job. I thought to my-self, 'Good God, I'm going to have to listen to this for the rest of my life!' I got up from the table and went upstairs and packed my things. I came out to Seattle and checked into the Marne Hotel. A while later a package arrived. She'd sent my things to me. When I opened the carton, packed on top of my clothes was a copy of Kipling's *The Light That Failed!* Oh, I don't know. This business of being 'happy' can get out of hand. When an artist marries, it certainly simplifies things if the other person has some feel for art and respects what you're trying to do."

I WAS TWENTY THEN, and in the emotional throes of an "I can't live with them and I can't live without them" impasse. My young friends were of little help. Most of them were usually in the same situation. I needed to know what Tobey would have to say, once he had heard me out. As usual, he said exactly what I needed to hear:

"Haven't you learned *yet* that *no* one is perfect?," he said, gently but very firmly. "When you love someone, you've got to be able to forgive *instantly.* You're going to be vulnerable. But it's our vulnerability that keeps us alive and sensitive to life. It's a very beautiful and important part of being human! You're young now. Don't, don't *ever* let that terrible thing called pride come between you and people you love! The sooner you learn this the better. And how many of us *never* learn it! Expect more from your work and yourself, and demand less from your friends. You just may find that your life is much the better for it!"

HENRY JAMES SAID, I believe, that most failures in art are not so much a matter of lack of talent as lack of character. For an artist who managed to accomplish so much, I marvel now at how much Tobey gave of himself to his friends. How often, in knocking on his door, I must have interrupted some painting he was working on. But I was knocking on his door because something was bothering me, and he was the one with whom I could best talk about it. He never said he was "too busy" if he sensed that my spirits were low and he might possibly be of some help.

Out of Nature:
Mark Tobey's Art

*"I am not an abstractionist—I am a humanist
and a naturalist."—Mark Tobey*

MY LONG FRIENDSHIP with Tobey began with our
weekly music lessons in Seattle in 1949 and soon led to
a friendship that would continue until my last visit to him several weeks before his death in Basel in 1976. We explored
art museums together, and during the 1950s Tobey and I often walked to the University of Washington's natural history
museum to look at rare and beautiful crystals, minerals, and
fossils. Tobey carefully studied their forms, textures, and colors. He was fascinated, for instance, by the many kinds of
blue one could see in lapis lazuli, azurite, and turquoise — or
the varying shades of red and orange in cinnabar, realgar, and
orpiment. We studied rutilated quartz crystals from Brazil.
Tobey pointed out to me how the slender, dark crystals of ru-
tile, penetrating in all directions the space of the clear quartz
crystal prisms, seemed to penetrate perspective. I was amazed

at the virtuosity of nature, at these intricate revelations of the artist's eye. In the Seattle Public Market we studied the vendors' displays of multicolored vegetables and fruits, the glint of light on the scales of freshly caught fish, or the tightly compacted energy in a drab-looking tulip bulb. Walking together in the arboretum we watched the trees and shrubs burst into bloom in the spring and later scatter their leaves as the winter came on.

Many artists throughout history have painted the four seasons — the singular and individual qualities of spring, summer, autumn, and winter. Vivaldi depicted them in music in his *The Four Seasons*. Tobey's *Edge of August* (1953), however, captures the essence of seasonal transition — the emphemerality of one season moving into the next. This painting is time and change made visible. French painter André Masson wrote, in a 1955 letter to Museum of Modern Art curator Alfred Barr: "Tobey's *Edge of August* is an astonishing masterpiece. The harmony between the inward being and nature — with life in its original state — without resorting to actual appearance on the one hand nor to geometric abstraction on the other. And with so much true conviction! I was bowled over by it!"

In his conversations with writer Selden Rodman, Tobey described his aim in painting this profoundly sensitive work: "*Edge of August* is trying to express the thing that lies between two conditions of nature — summer and fall. It's trying to capture that transition and make it tangible, make it sing. You might say that it's bringing the intangible into the tangible. In that sense, it's the opposite of an abstraction, though the means may appear abstract. To accomplish this aim, I used

Mark Tobey, sketching at the Pike Place Market, Seattle, 1946
(Photograph courtesy of the Seattle Times)

what symbols I had to. The mind and its associations were part of it."

"MY SOURCES OF INSPIRATION have gone from those of my native Middle West to those of microscopic worlds. I have discovered many a universe on paving stones and tree barks. I know very little about what is generally called 'abstract' painting. Pure abstraction would mean a type of painting completely unrelated to life, which is unacceptable to me."

TOBEY'S PAINTER'S EYE was omnivorous — it seemed to absorb everything. "Now there's something to look at!," he would exclaim with delight. It could be the sudden flash of whiteness against the winter grey sky as a seagull appeared above us. It could be an unusual configuration of clouds signaling an oncoming storm. Or it could be the various shapes of shadows cast by people and trees on a park lawn late in an autumnal afternoon. Nothing seemed to escape his attention — whether it was the phenomena of nature or the artifacts of modern civilization. It could even be a weathered scrap of newspaper in a gutter on Seattle's University Way. Or it could be the iridescent shimmer of an industrial oil film on a parking garage floor.

Mark Tobey did not "teach" me so much as he pointed out to me the multitudes of visual enchantments that comprise the intricate worlds of nature and the city. He understood the underlying unities of nature and society. To walk with him, partaking of his observations, was to discover as if for the first time the richness and variety of the visual world.

One could never be quite the same after having gone for a walk with Tobey down a city street with its teeming life of crowds and traffic or through a silent forest. No matter where he was, his restless painter's eye fed upon and devoured everything. Walking beside him, one knew that—silently, invisibly—new paintings were already being born in the stillness and privacy of his creative imagination. The transformation of nature into art had already begun.

Tobey repeatedly stressed, however, that although artists can draw their inspiration from nature, it is from art and other artists that they learn the language of art: "You just don't go to the country and paint—you learn from art and take that to the country with you. As Cézanne said, you have to bring much to nature. The French painters memorized the Louvre before they moved to the country to paint. Any painter who doesn't go through realism won't make it. My own so-called abstract paintings are the end result of a very long process that began in realism. I just don't believe for a moment that there are any shortcuts along the way! Each artist starts at the beginning and has to evolve in his own way."

BEHIND TOBEY'S OLD TWO-STOREY HOUSE on Brooklyn Avenue in Seattle's University District was a small garden. Sometimes he and I would sit on the back porch steps drinking our coffee. Next to us, growing beside the fence, was a hollyhock. Compared with the other plants and flowers in his backyard, this hollyhock seemed so inconspicuous. But the longer Tobey contemplated its tall, single stalk and closely appressed buds, the more possibilities he discovered in its abstract nature. "I didn't seek the vertical in the hollyhock—it was disclosed," he related to writer Selden Rodman. "I like best to see in nature what I want in my painting. I don't often enough. To do this, one must be in nature, awake and attentive. Then one must sleep—at least the conscious mind must sleep. Because if the resulting work is wholly conscious, it can't be true! When we can find the abstract *in nature* we find the deepest art. That is why the pictures growing out of tree forms in Mondrian's middle period are superior, for me anyway, to his later geometrical works." Tobey described to me how he painted: "I keep working on a painting, trying to get it to *feel* the way I want it to feel. Sometimes it comes out entirely different from what I started with. Other times I start not knowing what I'm going to do. Let other people come along and make a system out of it after it's finished!"

In 1990, fourteen years after Tobey's death, photographer Mary Randlett and I revisited Tobey's old house on Brooklyn Avenue. Part of the house still stood. The rest of it had been converted into the "Outrageous Taco," a fast-food restaurant. To our amazement, beside the backyard fence we found Tobey's solitary hollyhock still growing. Like his paintings, it was self-contained and majestic, the descendent of the self same hollyhock Tobey had contemplated some forty years earlier. It was the model for a dozen or more very abstract paintings: *Trio, Single Line, Space Line, The Snow-Woman,* and *Madame Push-Button,* to name a few. That same afternoon Mary Randlett and I visited the site of a large, old house on University Way. Tobey and his artist friend Pehr Hallsten had lived in this house during the late 1950s and early 1960s. Now a highrise apartment building stood in its place. In the alleyway behind the now-vanished house we found a few clematis vines still growing on the backyard fence, faint echoes of Tobey's garden of nearly half a century before. Those clematis flowers had become an abstract and mysterious presence in his painting *June Night*. Only a few of the neighboring buildings surrounding Tobey's houses had escaped urban renewal and the relentlessness of Progress. How strange, emblematic even, that what had survived were Tobey's inconspicuous plants, flowering at the edge of these changes.

I HAD ROUTINELY WRITTEN DOWN Tobey's remarks, many of which had to do with art, and often with nature:

"My friend Takesaki used to tell me, 'Let nature take over in your work. Get yourself out of the way when you paint.' But, as it is wisely said in Zen: 'You must be prepared before the fire can take over.' This is what I mean when I say that an artist should concentrate on his technique, so that he has a mastery of his craft. Then, when inspiration arrives, its expression will not be hampered by some lack of mastery of craft. Unless you know how to move your fingers on the piano, how to play the notes, how can you make music? But, mind you, you should develop your technique expressively."

"YOU MUST HAVE ROOTS. You have to care about things and be excited by them. Young artists want to be 'original' too soon, so they're afraid of being influenced. What they end up with is a few gimmicks, which they call their style. I was interested in everything when I was young. You can waste yourself trying to be original—that comes later. And don't squander your life trying to be your hometown's most fashionable painter! You just have to work and work and work until a real personality emerges."

"SOMETIMES I DON'T KNOW when to stop with a painting. At a point the mind starts to intrude, it wants to modify and change what you've done in the painting. You're on the verge of doing something different. The conscious mind wants to pull it back toward something you've already done. You've got to resist this sort of retreating! [Painter Albert Pinkham] Ryder described himself as an inchworm on the end of a branch, reaching into the air."

"ANYONE WHO TELLS YOU that the figure, landscape, and still life have had their day doesn't know what he's talking about — they're as good now for great painting as they ever were. But then I'm pretty old-fashioned in my attitudes, I guess. These days, if I were to paint what I want to, I'd paint the human figure. But I have this concern for space — and how do you reconcile the two in a picture? How many painters around us still draw from the model or still sketch from nature? No — they seem to think that these are things you stop doing when you leave art school. No wonder their paintings seem to have so little to do with life after a while. They haven't refreshed themselves before nature, before real things."

IN 1988 BETH SELLARS, curator of art at the Cheney Cowles Museum in Spokane, and I organized a Mark Tobey retrospective exhibition in anticipation of the 1990 Tobey centennial year. Many of the people who would attend that exhibition knew of Mark Tobey as a painter of abstract paintings — works that presumably had little to do with daily life, nature, or everyday sources in nature. For that reason, Sellars and I made a special point of trying to introduce the viewer to Tobey's roots in landscape, the figure, and still life — and in geological, botanical, and zoological inspiration. The exhibition included figurative works, landscapes, and still-life paintings done throughout his evolution as an artist, during his early and also his later years. Tobey obviously was an artist who practised what he preached.

The recurrent theme of nature in Tobey's work could easily be traced in the works included in the exhibition. *The Rock* (1934), three pastel and pencil drawings of moon snail shells (early 1940s), *Winter Growth* (1957), *Winter* (1961), *Earthen Field* (1961), *Summer Reflections* (1967), *Summer Breeze* (1970), *After Harvest* (1970), and *Morning Grass* (1975) documented the lifelong themes of nature and the changing seasons in Tobey's work.

Next to the exhibited works of art we installed glass cases containing natural objects from Tobey's personal collection — specimens now in the collections of the Burke Museum of Natural History and Culture in Seattle, Washington. Tobey's 1961 lithograph, *Winter*, resembled snow-white flakes falling from a winter-dark sky. But it also resembled the polished specimen of "snowflake obsidian" that Tobey had once owned, which was exhibited in one of the special cases of his private collection of minerals, seashells, corals, fossils, and crystals. We showed examples of polished petrified wood from Washington state and Arizona, fossil palm wood from Texas, brain coral from the Pacific Ocean, and polished agates and jasper from Mexico, Oregon, Wyoming, and Italy. Such specimens had become the starting point for many of Tobey's paintings. For example, the meandering lines and diffuse patches of color in Tobey's painting *Agate World* are very similar to the tracings of iron and manganese oxides in a semiprecious moss agate from the Oregon deserts. Tobey's ability to move from a natural object to a plastic realisation of that object — to the aesthetic formalization of nature — derives in part from his fluent sensitivity, as a pianist and music composer, to the qualities of musical texture and subtle shifts of tonality.

It was fascinating to watch the gallery viewers move back and forth, looking at these captivating objects from the world of natural history and then examining Tobey's so-called abstract paintings hanging on the nearby walls. It was all very well for Tobey to tell his students and friends: "I am not an abstractionist — I am a humanist and a naturalist." Here, the viewers could see for themselves the interplay between art and nature that lay at the heart of Tobey's exquisitely formal echoes and resonances of nature. Why, I asked myself, have so many other artists based works on similar sources so unsuccessfully? Why have their works so often seemed mechanically depictive, lifeless, illustrational — looking superficially like nature but somehow seeming neither natural nor alive? Tobey had gone past the surfaces of mere resemblance and had entered into the biological rhythms and endlessly rich diversities of life itself. He had found the abstract in nature while remaining entirely natural and in the spirit of nature.

Pehr Hallsten
& Mark Tobey

P EHR HALLSTEN painted his first picture in 1953, at the
age of fifty-six. Until then he had shown no particular interest in art, and he more or less tolerated classical music. He
was a scholar: fluent in at least seven or eight languages, an
incessant reader of philosophy and the classics. His world
consisted almost entirely of books.

When it came to making a living, he had somehow managed to do that by occasionally tutoring students in foreign
languages. Most of his life he had been poor as the proverbial
churchmouse, but he was blessed with a cheerful, optimistic,
and outgoing nature. He was exactly like his own paintings:
colorful and unpretentious.

Unlike Pehr, Mark Tobey did not have an aptitude for
foreign languages. He had spent the better part of his life trying to learn how to speak French, but he never could quite

get the hang of it. And this was how he met Pehr in the Ballard District of Seattle, around 1939.

Tobey's marriage had been a failure. When he proposed marriage a second time, he was turned down. By now he was lonely, at loose ends, and pretty much convinced that he was too involved with his painting to be a good provider and family man. He was charmed by Pehr's enthusiastic personality and erudition. They moved in together and continued to live together for twenty-five years.

Sometimes Tobey regretted not having made another attempt at marriage, for he loved children. But then he would say, "It's too late now to have any regrets. What's done is done. The family is sacred. If you have children, calling yourself an artist is no excuse for taking your family responsibilities lightly."

Tobey painted and Pehr read books. Tobey was very clear about the importance of Pehr's friendship and companionship: "It was Pehr who finally brought some stability into my life — a steady, dependable friend with whom I could live and still be able to get down to some serious painting for the first time in my life. We were so different from each other in so many ways. But we liked and respected each other, and that made the difference. Pehr didn't particularly 'understand' my pictures, but he was always so encouraging, and he respected my need to paint. I was very fortunate to meet him."

PEHR WAS CHRONICALLY, HOPELESSLY young, in the best sense of the word — an impish kid, sometimes a spoiled brat, but always one of the brightest spirits around, and a very good painter. In a way, he was Mark Tobey's alter ego.

Pehr Hallsten, Mark Tobey, and Wes Wehr, at Tobey's and Pehr's
house on University Way, Seattle, April 1962 (Photograph by Frank
Uchida, UW3877, courtesy of University of Washington Libraries)

In 1957 Thor V. Nyman, editor of the *Swedish Post* news-paper in Seattle, wrote an article about Pehr. He told about Tobey's encouraging Pehr to go back to school to complete his education. Nyman wrote, "At the age of fifty-six, just before he took up painting, Pehr completed a full college education in the record time of three years. For his University of Washington M.A. thesis he translated Strindberg's *Stora Landsvagen* (*The Chosen Highway*) — 'The Strindberg who was against himself, against his fellow men, and against God,' said Pehr."

SHORTLY AFTER PEHR BEGAN TO PAINT in 1953, I asked him, "Why did you suddenly start painting? You've never seemed interested in art."

"I don't know why. Maybe I'm like Topsy in the children's story — one day I just suddenly grew. Who knows why? I certainly don't!" He thought for a moment. "Oh, yes. Now I remember. Helmi had something to do with it." He was referring to Seattle painter Helmi Juvonen, his and Tobey's good friend.

Pehr continued, "Helmi used to drop by the little room I rented in the Kennedy Building on University Way. That was where I read in the afternoons while Mark was painting at our house up the street. Mark didn't want me around the house while he was working. When I'd watch Mark painting, it looked so difficult and complicated. But when Helmi painted, it looked so simple that even a clumsy oaf like me might be able to do it. I asked her to let me use some of her art materials. My first painting was of the building across the street from my Kennedy Building window — the picture you own. It came out far better than I expected."

Later I asked Helmi about this. In a letter to me, she responded: "I gave Pehr some Windsor and Newton watercolors and paper, for when he'd watched me paint he'd said he could paint too—it looked easy. The first things he painted were small, from memory. He had a good imagination and a good sense of color. He did some things from his Swedish childhood. Mark worked all day and had his evening classes. He and Pehr liked good food and liked to eat out."

Mark Tobey did not give Pehr "art lessons." He was very careful to let Pehr develop in his own way. Mostly he would tell Pehr, "Paint from your own heart—paint your memories, the things that catch your eye and have meaning for you." Tobey was concerned that Pehr might become self-conscious, explaining, "A watched pot never boils, and painters who are watched too much usually go to pot. Just before Feininger [painter Lyonel Feininger] died, he wrote me, 'For the first time in my life, I've become self-conscious.' This is a terrible thing for an artist—to be self-conscious. Then he's like the centipede that becomes aware of all its legs and starts tripping over them!"

PEHR'S WORK was already cut out for him when he began to paint. What a treasure trove of childhood memories he could draw upon. He had been born in Hammardalen, Jamtland, in northern central Sweden in 1897. Sometimes he described his vivid childhood memories to me—riding with the Lapps in their sleighs in the dead of winter, the whiteness of the snow, the stained-glass window colors of those fierce Nordic sunsets, and all the wonderful stories the Lapps told him—of trolls and witches and magic spells. I think there was something in Pehr that never quite left him, that he brought

with him to America in the 1920s, a part of him that somehow
believed that just perhaps—after all, who *really* knows?—
there were indeed *real* trolls in those northern forests of his
childhood? And maybe, sometimes when things didn't go
very well, just maybe there were *real* witches who did cast evil
spells? One thing I'm sure of: Pehr never "outgrew" his rich
heritage.

Pehr would often phone me, asking if I would like to
have lunch with him at Manning's on University Way. Or perhaps we could take a taxi cab to another part of town for
lunch. Pehr had started painting for the first time in 1953. I
liked his paintings very much and had begun to collect them.
I asked him about his work.

"I'm not an important painter. Mark is, but I'm not. It's
very nice that people like my little pictures and want to buy
so many of them. But I'm like the parsley on the plate. I'm not
the meat and potatoes. I'm just a dash of color and something
a little different on the sidelines. And even my name, Pehr,
is a little different too," he answered.

In his own way, Pehr Hallsten was a worldly and sophisticated man, gallant and quite at home in the most elegant
restaurants and hotels in Europe and New York. He could be
courtly and suave, but he hated pomposity and people who put
on airs. He was something of a snob himself. He knew when
things had quality and when they didn't. He could be bitingly
sarcastic when anything was pretentious or poorly done.

Pehr didn't like to talk much about his work, but now and
then he might mention it: "The winters in Sweden were long
and gloomy. It was dark so much of the time. I think that may
be partly why we Northerners like and need bright colors—

why the traditional costumes have so much color, and the interiors of the houses have so much brightly painted furniture. It's just a way of making life a little more cheerful.

"Most of us are rather like the trolls I often paint — sometimes a little wicked, and sometimes rather kind. None of us, when it comes down to it, is really either a great saint or a great sinner. We're somewhere in between. A little bit of both. That's perhaps one of the hardest things for most of us to accept about ourselves — how in between and alike we are."

PEHR AND TOBEY left Seattle during the early 1960s to settle in Basel, Switzerland. Their seventeenth-century house on Saint Albans Vorstad was large and drafty. The Basel winters were gloomy and could seem to go on forever. After a time, Pehr would become restless and irritable. He'd be acutely homesick for Stockholm, or anxious to go south for the winter — to Spain, or Italy, or back to Palma on Majorca. Almost anywhere. Like many Nordics, he longed for the Mediterranean climates. Tobey was busy preparing exhibitions and had to concentrate on his work. Pehr was bored by the daily routines and oppressive winters in Basel. Tempers would flare up until Pehr and Tobey were at swords' point.

Finally Pehr would take off on his own. He roamed about Europe, writing hundreds of postcards from Madrid, Rome, Stockholm, Palma, the Balearic Isles. It was impossible to keep track of him. He sent us exotic little souvenirs: a snapshot of himself standing next to painter Joan Miro in Palma, or sitting proudly in a horse-drawn carriage somewhere in Italy. In every snapshot he grinned triumphantly at the camera. His neatly written messages were filled with the names of all his "charming new friends." Pehr was gregarious. He met people easily and, almost without exception, he charmed everyone he met.

Pehr had a diabetic attack in Rome and, through a mix-up with the local officials who thought he was drunk, ended up in a Roman prison surrounded by thugs, thieves, and murderers. Notified in Basel, Tobey was in a panic. Pehr thought the whole episode was great fun. When he was released, he promptly wrote a somewhat unprintable account of the experience.

Pehr's motto was *carpe diem*: live for the moment. Tobey, hard at work in Basel, would fret and worry constantly about Pehr's disregarding his doctors' orders and abusing his health. Pehr was diabetic, but he just couldn't resist pastries and candies. He wasn't supposed to smoke, either. But off on his own, without Tobey to keep an eye on him, Pehr would live it up on the grand scale. He thumbed his nose at the doctors' orders and warnings. In near desperation, Tobey would complain to me, "I can't live with him and I can't live without him! When he's here, I can't concentrate. He needs so much attention all the time. When he's away, I worry myself to death that he's not taking care of himself." But eventually Pehr would return to Basel and settle back into the old routines. Tobey would paint, and Pehr would read, and their life together would become tranquil again.

No matter where he was, Pehr was irrepressible. The Lowell Dining Room on Capitol Hill comes to mind. It was a staid and rather demure restaurant, with an old-fashioned hush about it. One afternoon Pehr, painter Erich Thrun, and I went there for a quiet lunch. We sat reading our menus. We were properly dressed and so well-behaved that no one noticed us. An attractive, matronly woman came to take our order. She was plump. Her well-groomed hair was tinted lavender. Pehr studied her intently.

"*You* look like a woman with a *past* — a *wonderful* past! *Everyone* should have a past. I'll wager that yours was *very* romantic!"

The hostess turned beet-red. She was embarrassed, but delighted. She barely managed to write down our orders and then fled toward the kitchen. A few minutes later she returned, a bit formal and seemingly composed. The three of us, Pehr, Erich, and I, had ordered Swedish meatballs. She placed our entrees before us, winked wickedly at Pehr and left the room. Pehr immediately noticed that there was one more meatball on his plate than on ours. He was gleeful. "Ah, she likes me! And I like her, too! When I like people I let them know it. But I try to do it in a nice way. I have to play the clown and fool at times just to brighten things up a bit. If you two boys weren't so shy and self-conscious you could have so much more fun. How many love letters do either of you receive each week? I receive *lots* of them, and I'm an old man. What? You two don't receive any at all! There's obviously something very wrong. Listen to Pehr, if you like people there's no harm in *telling* them so. They like to hear it, *if* you know how to say it nicely. And sometimes it can lead to some very romantic and wonderful things! When I like someone, I *tell* them so. When Mark likes someone, he just gets complicated about it."

Tobey had been very supportive of Pehr during their lean years in Seattle. Now, in the late 1950s and until he died in 1965, Pehr was successful and relatively solvent for the first time in his life. His exhibitions in New York and Paris, and with Seattle dealers Otto Seligman and Francine Seders, were well received. There were glowing reviews by John Ashbery, Michel Courtois, Dore Ashton, and others. Collectors of his work included uranium tycoon and art collector Joseph Hirshhorn and actor Vincent Price. English painter Ben Nicholson and the Portuguese painter Vieira da Silva bought work by Pehr during his 1961 show at the Galerie Jeanne Bucher in Paris. Dr. Richard E. Fuller, founder and director of the Seattle Art Museum, bought one of his watercolors, *Young Life No. 1* (1962), for the museum's permanent collection and included Pehr in the 1962 Seattle World's Fair exhibition of Northwest Art.

In 1961, Pehr was invited by Gordon Washburn, director of the Carnegie Institute in Pittsburgh, to exhibit in the Carnegie's 1961 International. His work was so well received that in 1962 he was invited to have a one-man exhibit at the Carnegie Institute. Washburn had high praise for the exhibit. In a July 5, 1962, letter to Mark Tobey he wrote, "We have just put the Pehr show on our walls and are absolutely enchanted by it. After it was hung I walked in the room and felt my spirit leap with pleasure at the sight of the beautiful colors and the force of the images. There is a real greatness in Pehr which makes itself felt even at a distance. They are even more engaging at close range, and we have been looking at them over and over again with profound satisfaction."

Colin Graham, now director emeritus of the Art Gallery of Greater Victoria, British Columbia, recognized the distinctiveness of Pehr's work and gradually assembled the first comprehensive collection of Pehr's paintings to be owned by any museum. In 1974, the museum published an illustrated catalog of Pehr's works in its collection.

In his 1961 introduction to Pehr's exhibition at the Galerie Jeanne Bucher in Paris, Tobey wrote: "With some encouragement the paintings flowed forth from his childhood memories reminding me of my own, although his was spent in unforgettable realms of reindeer, Lapps and snow, nights of darkness where trolls stole the light of day and Baldur was slain by an arrow made of mistletoe. As he continued, strange birds appeared and his people came from out of the past in garments of beautiful colour. In an age of abstractions I have always found Pehr's work appealing and marveled at his colour sense. His paintings came from himself and of that which his ancestors bequeathed him in the early days when the world about him spread a magic carpet for his imagination."

Pehr died from diabetic complications in Basel in 1965. During the summer of 1967 Tobey was in Seattle for what was to be his last visit. Unexpectedly he said, "You know, Wes, my friendship with Pehr went so deep that at times perhaps not much of it showed on the surface. But when I die, the first friend I will want to see again will be Pehr. Very few people every really knew him or understood him. But he was a remarkable man, and my gratitude to him is enormous."

Helmi Juvonen:
The Nordic Pearl

URING THE MISERABLY rainy winter of 1950, I
worked on weekends as a guard at the Henry Art Gallery
on the University of Washington campus. My job was very
simple: I sat at a desk in an office adjoining the main entrance.
From there I could observe everyone who came and went. It
was one of my responsibilities to keep track of gallery atten-
dance by clicking a counter device every time anyone came
through the front door. Gallery visitors were few and far between. Gallery security was minimal, even though Horace
Henry's collection of paintings by Corot, Delacroix, Boudin,
Bouguereau, Inness, Daubigny, Homer, and others hung in
the next room. It never worried the staff that thieves or van-
dals might visit the gallery. That sort of thing simply never
happened.

One Saturday afternoon a woman strode quickly through

the front door and into the museum office carrying two shopping bags. She wore a brightly flowered blouse and skirt. Her clothes were Nordic and peasantlike in their hand-embroidered simplicity. It was difficult to guess this rather strange woman's age. Her voice, high-pitched and excitable, was childlike. She introduced herself to me quickly and efficiently. Her name was Helmi Juvonen. Helmi was the Finnish word for pearl. Both her parents had been Finnish immigrants. But everyone called her Helmi. She was an artist. Was I a painter, too? Did I know Mark? Morris? She meant Mark Tobey and Morris Graves, I assumed. Yes, I had just met them, I told her.

Helmi began to unwrap some of the ceramics that were in her two shopping bags. They were carefully wrapped in newspapers. She had just delivered some of her handmade ash trays and keychains to Dorothy's Gift Shop in the Olympic Hotel downtown, she told me. Helmi watched me carefully as I examined each of the ceramics. She noticed that I seemed to like especially an ashtray with a boldly incised thunderbird design on it. It was much more attractive than the generic black plastic ashtray I used on the gallery desk. "You like this one, don't you? I can tell. I want you to have it," she said, handing it to me. "I'm a very practical person," she explained. "I've always known how to make a living as an artist, one way or another. People like my ashtrays and key chains. I sell lots of them in gift shops around town."

Helmi was forty-seven years old when I met her that afternoon. She was born in Butte, Montana, on January 17, 1903. At the age of fifteen, she moved to Seattle with her mother and sister and attended Queen Anne High School, majoring in home economics. Upon graduation, she was awarded two art scholarships to the Cornish Art Institute in Seattle. During the 1938–1940 Federal Arts Project, Helmi studied lithography with Emilio Amero and began to do linoleum-cut prints based on Northwest Coast Indian subject matter. During World War II she was employed as a draftsman by the Boeing Aircraft Company and attended night classes at the University of Washington, studying mechanical drawing under Hiram Chittenden. Unlike Mark Tobey, who was very analytical when he commented on paintings, Helmi rarely spoke about art in technical terms. She gave every appearance of being something of a primitive artist, when she was, in fact, an artist with considerable technical training and skill.

During the 1951 Bon Odori festival, Helmi sat on the front steps of the Buddhist Temple in Seattle's International District sketching the dancers and people in the audience. This annual Buddhist festival honors deceased ancestors and celebrates the oneness of life. The sketches she made during that summer evening were later incorporated into a large painting entitled *Bon Odori*, now in the collection of the Seattle Art Museum.

She traveled throughout Washington, sketching people and their cultures. In 1953 she traveled to Neah Bay on the Olympic Peninsula to sketch the Makah Indian dances and costumes. In Yakima she recorded the Yakama Indian ceremonies. Near Bellingham, she attended the Lummi-Swinomish tribal dances. One of her most famous prints, *Winter Dance Time* (1945–46), records this sacred ceremony. During 1951–53 she did hundreds of drawings and paintings based on the Native American objects in the old Washington State Museum on the campus. These artifacts are now in the

*Helmi Juvonen, printmaking at the Washington State Museum
(now, the Burke Museum) on the University of Washington campus,
early 1950s (Photograph courtesy of the* Seattle Times*)*

collections of the newly renamed Burke Museum of Natural History and Culture at the University of Washington.

Although Helmi knew personally such noted anthropologists as Erna Gunther and Viola Garfield, she was not herself a professionally trained anthropologist. As an artist, however, she had a keen eye for observing and drawing the tribal dance movements, costumes, and regalia. Many of the sketches she made during the 1940s and 1950s would later be of considerable historical and ethnological importance. Her sketches of the Makah dances, costumes, and tribal objects constitute one of the few surviving records of Makah ceremonies from that time. Dr. Richard E. Fuller, founder and director of the Seattle Art Museum, was a crucial source of continuing patronage and encouragement. Fuller bought many of Helmi's major works for the Seattle Art Museum's permanent collection.

Although she lived in a small house at Alki Point when first I met her in 1950, Helmi sojourned almost daily on University Way, sketching just about everyone and everything she saw. Her sketch books were filled with the names and addresses of the countless people she met from one day to the next. She was outgoing and gregarious, and she loved to meet new people. Nonetheless, in that she never married and never had a regular companion of any sort, she was essentially a loner.

In the early 1950s Helmi moved to the University District. For a while she lived above John Uitti's frame shop on 43rd Avenue, at a busy corner of University Way. At the entrance to John's shop, she hung a clothesline, on which each morning she pinned her newest linoleum blockprints. "Original block prints, 50 cents each. Please leave money in tin can. Thank you!" read her neatly printed sign. Her prints always sold briskly. No one, it seemed, was so broke that he couldn't afford a print or two at Helmi's prices. Besides, her clothesline exhibition was at the entrance to John's shop. Dozens of people — framing customers and artists alike — came and went through that door every day. By evening Helmi could count on finding the tin can full of coins and dollar bills. "This is much more money than I really need!" she insisted. If Helmi spotted artist Bob West and me on University Way, she invariably filled our pockets with coins, saying, "Here, you boys buy yourselves a good lunch. The two of you are so thin. You both look like you could use a square meal!"

On Saturday afternoons during the 1950s, Helmi exhibited and sold her works in a rented stall in the Seattle Public Market. Her prints were so reasonably priced and sold so well that her weekend sales often provided her with enough money to get comfortably through the rest of the week. I ran into her on the street around 1954 or so. "Where are you headed, Helmi?"

"I'm on my way to the art store to buy some Windsor and Newton white tempera paint. It gives my pictures that spooky quality people like so much," she explained. Helmi's fantasy paintings were as much about spooks and goblins and things that go bump in the night as they were about mystical matters. And yet she was one of the most down-to-earth artists I have ever known.

"Mon Sweet Mark, I am busy painting pictures for our big exhibition so we can make lots of money and get hitched. Pablo Picasso can be our best man. Just remember — feather beds are best. Love toujours, Helmi."

HELMI'S OBSESSION with artist Mark Tobey reached epic proportions during the mid-1950s. Before that, her hero-worship for Tobey had been relatively restrained. Tobey had always advised the artists around him to "paint out of your own life!" Helmi certainly did exactly that. Tobey appeared in every imaginable role in her paintings and prints. The Nordic Heritage Museum owns a watercolor entitled *Tobey in the Sauna*. It depicts a red-faced, embarrassed Mark Tobey, wearing only his long-johns while naked nymphs cavort around him in the sauna. In other paintings Tobey appears as Jesus. Or there are the depictions of the happily married Helmi and Tobey surrounded by hundreds of their offspring. *Tobey Enters University Way*, a variation on James Ensor's *Christ Enters Brussels*, depicted Tobey striding down the center of University Way. Behind Tobey followed his faithful flock of admirers — and just about any of the other artists and habitués Helmi could think of who were on University Way at that time.

Years later, looking through a portfolio of her works that Helmi kept in her closet at the Oakhurst Convalescent Center (in Elma, Washington, a small town between Olympia and Aberdeen), I found a small watercolor sketch. It was Mark Tobey, beard and all. But he was wearing a Helmi-like dress. I didn't know what to make of it. Helmi piped, "That's Mark. Sometimes he acted like a little old lady. So I painted him like one!"

Tobey was mortified by Helmi's obsession with him. She even went so far as to make a linoleum print depicting herself and Tobey as a happily wedded couple. "Tobey will be wed," it proclaimed. It was her handmade wedding announcement.

She mailed it everywhere — to art museum directors, to art critics, and to famous fellow artists in New York and Europe. Helmi had made up her mind. Tobey and she were meant for each other. It only remained for Tobey to come to his senses and realize this too, which never happened.

DURING THE 1950S, there were frequent public complaints about some of Helmi's social behavior. She had already had periods of being institutionalized. Anthropologist Ruth Benedict, in her classic work *Patterns of Culture*, had put her finger on the problem. The central problem in American social life, as Benedict explained, was the public fear of anything or anyone who was in any way "different." Helmi's "individualism" was considered "socially inappropriate" by the medical profession. Even though Helmi was a social terror at times, she was institutionalized at a point in our history when just about anyone could be locked up for just about anything that deviated from convention. Individualism was, it seemed, a threat to "traditional values." In this regard, Helmi was decades ahead of her time. By the 1970s, individualism would be considered almost the norm.

In March 1960, Helmi was made a ward of the state. For the remaining twenty-five years of her life she shared a large room with several other patients at the Oakhurst Convalescent Center in Elma. She continued to draw and paint, but her works were rarely exhibited in Seattle. Now and then the Henry Art Gallery and the Seattle Art Museum might exhibit one of her works from their permanent collections. Each year, however, she painted a large work for the Grays Harbor County Fair art show, which was held about a mile down the road from Oakhurst. Helmi could always count on winning a blue ribbon for her entry.

In 1975, art patrons Anne Gould Hauberg and Betty Bowen organized an exhibition of Helmi's work at the Pacific Northwest Arts Center in Pioneer Square. Collector Robert Sarkis photographed Helmi with *Seattle Times* art critic Deloris Tarzan and several schoolchildren who had come up from Elma with Helmi to see the show. Helmi's old friend Ivar Haglund hosted lunch for her at Ivar's Acres of Clams. The restaurant was only a few blocks away from the gallery, and we all walked there together. At lunch, two of our most colorful local personalities, Helmi and Ivar, sat side by side, affectionately holding hands. Ivar now had a successful, even world-famous restaurant chain. (The irony of this, as poet Nelson Bentley wrote in his poem, "A Classical Elegy for Ivar Haglund," is that Tobey had many years earlier advised Haglund, "Don't try to open a restaurant, Ivar. You should play the guitar.")

The Pioneer Square exhibition marked the beginning of Helmi's return from creative seclusion. The director of the Frye Art Museum, Mrs. Walser (Kay) Greathouse, invited me to guest curate a large show of Helmi's work. I assumed that the Frye show would consist solely of earlier work. Not at all. Helmi announced: "I'm going to have a big show at a museum in Seattle. I have to get back to work and paint lots of new pictures."

During the following months a flood of new work appeared as Helmi plunged into painting again. She was like someone possessed! Northwest Coast totemic masks and petroglyphs, paintings of children frolicking under apple trees in an orchard, cats and kittens dancing around Mark Tobey, spooky-looking birds and fishes—the new work was not only inventive but wholly unpredictable! During the months while Helmi was getting ready for her show at the Frye, one of the Oakhurst patients innocently asked her if she wouldn't like to join some of the other patients in the television room next to the main lobby. Helmi snapped at her, "Turn that thing off! Why don't you people do something *constructive?*" Helmi's nurses at Oakhurst reported to me that her health had suddenly improved and she just didn't seem to have time to complain. She was much too busy painting for her show.

I often visited Helmi while she was preparing for the Frye Museum exhibition. She wrote to me when she had just finished a new batch of works for the show, asking me to please come down and pick them up. During one such visit, Helmi and I went outside to sit in a sheltered area where she often sketched during the afternoon and played with her kitty cats. "That's Mrs. Dill Pickle," exclaimed Helmi, pointing at a very pregnant cat. "She enjoys having babies. She has them all the time! She keeps me busy coming up with names for each of them and remembering which kitty cat is which." Two elderly men shuffled by us. They appeared to be patients at Oakhurst. One of the men was slovenly. His shirt was not tucked into his pants. Helmi chastised him in undisguised disgust. "Tuck your shirt in! Just because we're here is no excuse for not taking pride in your appearance."

On November 16, 1976, Helmi arrived for the opening of her retrospective at the Frye Art Museum. Mrs. Greathouse came forward to meet her. She was enchanted by Helmi's exhibition. She was also very curious about Helmi. How did she arrange having her shows? Was it time-consuming?

"Oh, I just leave all of that to Wes," answered Helmi. "He knows what's best for me!"

They started to talk about Helmi's pictures. "Helmi, tell me, what do you paint with?"

"Oh, anything anybody gives me," responded Helmi brightly.

And this was true. She was eager to try out different kinds of papers, or new pigments. She often wrote to many of her friends asking that we send her a certain brand of oil pastel or watercolor, or more pads of watercolor paper, or it might be a certain anthropological or art book. If she needed shoes, Helmi sent us a pencil tracing of both her feet. Since she sent identical requests to so many different friends, when I visited at Oakhurst I often found her room stacked high with duplicate copies of books she needed, or with numerous sets of the art materials. Finally an Oakhurst nurse took me aside. "Helmi has lots of clothes and things. She writes to everyone as if she doesn't have anything at all. She just likes to get packages in the mail. Waiting for the mailman gives her something to look forward to," the nurse explained.

At the opening, a tall, well-dressed, older man stepped toward us, his hand extended to Helmi. Before he could say anything, Helmi welcomed him with delight, "You look like somebody *very* important. Are you?" The man never explained who he was (or what he did for a living), but he too was instantly captivated by Helmi.

Painter Glenn Brumett and I escorted Helmi slowly around the exhibition, so that she could have some time to look at the works. "Oh, I like that painting!" she exclaimed, pointing to one of her earlier works. "Who painted it?"

"You did!" Glenn replied, smiling.

"I did? Well, I *still* like it!"

Helmi seemed to have no narcissistic attachment to her own work. But its subject matter could delight her—when it reminded her of something she liked. When she spotted one of her cat paintings on the wall, Helmi exclaimed, "There are my kitty cats! I've painting them lots of times! I hope somebody remembered to feed them. I'm going to get home long after their usual dinner time."

Helmi was pleased with her Frye Museum exhibition. I asked her when she had painted a certain picture, an early tempera from perhaps around 1953 or so? "But Pumpkin, that was so *long* ago! I can't remember when I did do that one. It doesn't really matter, anyway," she responded. (While perhaps frustrating to the curator or archivist, Helmi's ability to ignore the calendar freed her to focus intensely on the present. Over time, I would continue to ask her for clues as to when she had painted various of her works. Her answer was invariably the same: "I never paid much attention to dates, and they don't mean anything to me now!") She was clearly not interested in living in the past. But she was most interested in the frames on her pictures: "Who framed my pictures? Is he here today? I want to meet whoever it was and thank him." More and more people kept coming up to Helmi to congratulate her. Helmi charmed everyone who met her that afternoon. Her effortless wit and lack of self-importance were wonderful. A few moments later, when they were alone together, Helmi whispered to Glenn Brumett, "Pumpkin (she called anyone she liked "Pumpkin"), how am I doing? I'm so used to talking to idiots that I've forgotten how to talk to normal people!"

THE BURKE MUSEUM exhibition of the Marshall and Helen Hatch collection of Helmi works (1982); and exhibitions at the Nordic Heritage Museum (1984); the Washington State Capitol Museum (1984) and the Evergreen State College Art Galleries (1984), the latter two in Olympia; the Whatcom Museum of History and Art in Bellingham (1985); and the Cheney Cowles Museum in Spokane (1986) introduced a large public to Helmi's works, many of which had never before been exhibited. These museum shows, however, were no mere ego trip for Helmi. For her they were mainly occasions for seeing a lot of old and new friends again at all the openings and special parties given in her honor. Ivar Haglund, John and Alma Uitti, Gary Lundell, Jean Russell, Helen Blackwood, Jo and Julian Jenner, Gervais Reed, Priscilla Chong, and many, many such friends were at the museum door to greet her when she arrived with her friend Brent Goeres from Elma. When the treasures of the "King Tut" exhibition came to Seattle during 1978, Brent brought Helmi to the city for the afternoon. Helmi was predictably most delighted by the Egyptian cat statues in the exhibition. When Jean Russell invited Helmi to spend the night at Jean's apartment on Queen Anne hill, offering to drive her back to Elma the following day, Helmi replied, "Oh, no. But thank you very much anyway. I do have to get home tonight. My kitty cats will be waiting for their dinner. They'll wonder what's happened to me if I don't show up!"

HELMI ALWAYS MADE a memorable entrance at her exhibition openings. She invariably wore a brightly colored dress, one that she had sewed and embroidered. For these special occasions she placed a bright bit of colored yarn, usually pink, in her hair. Sometimes, when Brent arrived at Oakhurst to pick her up for an opening, Helmi was still preoccupied with trying to decide just what she should wear. She was trying on various of her hats, most of which she had designed and made herself. One hat in particular did not at all meet her exacting standards. She flung it on the floor angrily, exclaiming in sheer disgust, "This hat isn't fit to wear to a dog race!" Besides bringing her to Seattle from Elma for these openings, Brent kept a close eye on Helmi at home, visiting her at Oakhurst, taking her for drives in the country, bringing her art supplies, and making sure that she was all right. Driving back to Elma with Brent after one such occasion, Helmi happily exclaimed to him, "I may be an old lady now, but I've never had so much fun in my life!"

IN 1983 MARIANNE FORSSBLAD, director of the Nordic Heritage Museum in Ballard, invited me to guest curate a large exhibition of Helmi's work. When the exhibition opened in 1984, Mrs. Forssblad hosted a reception for Helmi at the museum. Kay Greathouse came to the party. Arnold Jollas, director of the Seattle Art Museum, was also there. The two had never met. "Arnold, would you like to meet Kay Greathouse?" I asked him, "That's impossible!" he answered. "She *never* returns my phone calls. I've invited her to lunch. She doesn't answer my letters. Just how do you imagine I could ever meet her at that rate?"

"She's standing right behind you!"

Arnold turned around to find himself facing Kay Greathouse.

"Kay, I would like to introduce you to Arnold Jollas," I said.

"Not *the* Mr. Jollas?" asked Kay.

"Just one of *many*, ma'am," answered Arnold, bowing elegantly and extending his hand.

With that, I made an exit. When I came back into the room a little while later, Kay and Arnold were still talking. They had hit it right off. The party was such a festive and happy occasion for Helmi that she decided to make the Nordic Heritage Museum the "official repository" for her ceramics, jewelry, embroideries, figurines, and some of her original blocks.

HELMI'S EXHIBITION OPENINGS usually attracted many people from the Seattle art community, including people who generally would not have chosen to be in the same place at the same time. Museum directors, curators, rival dealers, art critics, and collectors who were not always on the friendliest of terms mingled convivially at Helmi's previews and receptions. They were finally able to meet one another on "neutral ground." Helmi often became the great social equalizer.

Art collector and patron Jean Russell was a faithful collector and champion of the work of many Pacific Northwest artists—Phillip McCracken, Jay Steensma, Joseph Goldberg, Richard Gilkey, Paul Dahlquist, Gary Lundell, and others. She also had a station wagon. This was especially important to me because I neither owned a vehicle nor had ever learned how to drive one. On weekends, Jean, artist Gary Lundell, and I often drove to Elma to take Helmi out for the afternoon. We usually drove to the nearby town of Rochester, where there was a small restaurant Helmi especially liked. Nestled in the Chehalis Valley, Rochester was about twenty miles south of Elma. Sometimes we stopped on the road along the way, near the towns of Porter and Malone. After a rain storm, the cliffs beside the road glistened with brilliant white fossil shells from a time, some thirty or so million years earlier, when this area had been an ocean floor. Gary and I were busy looking for the concretions that often contained fossil crabs. Helmi enjoyed "beach-combing" for the fossil shells weathering out of the hillside along the country road. Once Jean, Gary, and I took Helmi to the coast for a picnic on the beach at Westport. For Helmi this was a great adventure — to see the ocean again. She took off her shoes and socks and very cautiously waded in the tidal surf, bending over now and then to pick up a shell or bit of brightly colored kelp.

At the small cafe in Rochester, Helmi studied the menu carefully. She usually came to the same conclusion: "Ice cream is always good, and soup is very nourishing." She ordered simple things. Her real delight, however, was the cellophane-wrapped soda crackers. She stuffed her skirt pockets with them. Helmi usually ordered such plain fare in restaurants that Brent and I finally decided it was high time she savor some real cuisine. At Hoquiam, a half-hour's drive west of Elma, we knew of a restaurant that served delicious but somewhat pricey meals. We took Helmi there for dinner, and Brent urged her to try the specialty, an elaborately prepared chicken dish. It was wildly expensive, of course, but Brent and I didn't let Helmi know this. The entree arrived. Helmi tasted a little of it. "This is very nice. My kitty cats love chicken. They can have the rest of this for dinner." After that, Brent and I resumed taking Helmi to less elegant eating places.

One afternoon, when Jean, Gary, and I brought Helmi back to Oakhurst after an outing in the Chehalis Valley, a tall, stately woman bore down upon us—a bit slow, a bit wobbly, but decidedly imperious. She had dressed elaborately in black and was wearing some gaudy and obviously fake diamonds. She was a patient at Oakhurst, but she behaved like a dowager duchess. When she saw Helmi coming through the door, she pulled me aside, annoyed. "Why did you have to bring *her* back? Helmi acts like she owns this place. She's always bossing us around. I wish you'd left her back in town!"

DURING THE LATE 1960S, Gary Lundell and I drove to Elma with two staff members from the Henry Art Gallery. Director LaMar Harrington had just initiated the oral history program for the Archives of Northwest Art. We taped part of an interview with Helmi while driving to Rochester for lunch. "Helmi," I asked her, "tell me about suffering artists."

"Suffering artists? I don't know *what* you're talking about!" she protested. "Artists have *wonderful* lives. They can do all sorts of things normal people can't do."

Gary asked her how she had managed to make ends meet during the lean years of the Great Depression. "I did just fine," she said. "I figured out there would always be things people needed, even when the times were bad—things like ashtrays, place mats, and party favors. So I made lots of practical things like that. When I studied at Cornish, Miss Cornish taught us to be practical if we wanted to be artists."

Helmi was not interested in gossip of any sort. She disliked "snoopy" people. It was rare for her to say anything even mildly critical about anyone, let alone to be sarcastic. If she didn't like some individuals, she didn't show it directly. She merely tuned them out politely. Her opinions of other artists were simply stated: "Morris has lots of imagination. I like most of what he paints." A few lines such as these pretty much summed up what Helmi had to say about Morris Graves's work. She could never have survived for a moment as a newspaper or journal art critic. Her opinions of other painters were far too succinct to fill up the necessary columns of print in a newspaper review. I can't recall that she ever made any specific or technical criticisms of the work we young painters showed her. When I did bring my work to Elma, she looked through it silently, studying each painting or drawing carefully. "I like these especially," she would announce finally, singling out several of the works. Henry Art Gallery editor Joseph Newland and I decided that we should, while we still could, try to have Helmi document some of her own work. We made up an album of xeroxes of many of her 1950s linoleum prints and showed her the images for her comment. Helmi turned the pages, looking at the works in a somewhat detached way. "That's nice!" she said of one print. "I rather like that one," she said of another print. If the print did nothing for her, she merely looked at it for a moment and went on to the next page.

For the most part, Helmi was a loner. But though she spent most of her time working on her art, she did know a good number of the local painters. Helmi and artist Pehr Hallsten liked each other. For one thing, they were both Scandinavian. During the early 1950s Helmi often visited Pehr at the small room in the Kennedy Building on University Way where he read and painted during the afternoons, while his companion Mark Tobey painted in his studio down the street. In fact, it was Helmi who first started Pehr painting in 1953.

Morris Graves, too, was genuinely fond of Helmi and wrote her often, although only a few of his letters to her still survive. Many of Graves's postcards and letters to her were later stolen, she wrote him. He even made a visit to her at Oakhurst with art patron and collector Marshall Hatch. Guy Anderson knew her only slightly. Tobey, especially during the worst years of Helmi's spectacular obsession with him, was scared to death of how she might next embarrass him. Oddly enough, I don't recall that painter Jay Steensma and Helmi ever met—even though I used to tell Jay that if Tobey and Helmi had married, as Helmi insisted they should have, their love-child could well have been a painter like Jay.

HELMI LAID CLAIM to a remarkable set of correspondents, but no matter how unlikely it might have seemed at the time, it invariably turned out she knew what she was talking about. If she said she had just received a letter from Queen Elizabeth, or from President Lyndon Johnson and his daughter Lynda, she most likely *had* just heard from them. She wrote to anyone and everyone. The king and queen of Spain sent her a Christmas card. Nelson Rockefeller wrote to her. If she was going to be confined at Oakhurst, she might just as well write to people everywhere and see to it that her mailbox was never empty. Helmi and I were very much alike in that regard—we both liked to receive lots of letters and to write them. Waiting for the mailman to arrive gave each of us something to look forward to from one day to the next, especially during the long, rainy winters in the Pacific Northwest. I liked the way Helmi routinely ended her letters, advising the recipient to "Eat lots of nutritious food, be cheerful, and keep busy!" It took me many years to realize that Helmi was giving first-rate advice.

In 1979 filmmaker Kenneth Levine produced a documentary entitled *Northwest Visionaries* which included footage on eight Northwest artists: Mark Tobey, Morris Graves, Guy Anderson, George Tsutakawa, Kenneth Callahan, Margaret Tomkins, Paul Horiuchi, and Helmi Juvonen. This documentary contains the only known motion-picture footage of Helmi. Photographed at Oakhurst, she is shown sketching, surrounded by her cats. Unfortunately, this drab footage gives no idea whatsoever of Helmi's creative vitality and the independence of her life even while she was confined at Oakhurst. The background commentary characterizes her as having "a personality deficiency"—another cliche during those years for describing people who didn't toe the conventional line.

Shortly after this film was first aired, *Seattle Times* art critic Deloris Tarzan and I drove to Elma to visit Helmi. We had lunch with her at the truck-stop cafe across the road. Dee asked Helmi her age. Helmi refused to answer such a "personal" question. Dee, being a first-rate investigative reporter, was not one to take silence for an answer. She started asking questions in a roundabout way, "Now, Helmi, you went to Queen Anne High School when? Which year?"

Helmi knew very well what Dee was up to. "I know what reporters are like. I know their tricks when they want to find out something. After all, I *did* write the gossip column for the *Seattle Times*, you know. I am *not* going to tell you how old I am. That's my secret. Why, I imagine not even Wes knows how old I am." But all credit goes to the local newspaper reporters, who were proud of having a famous artist and personality such as Helmi in their midst. She was a colorful individual—what the journalists call "good copy." They apparently had found out what Dee could not, for as she stood in the Oakhurst hallway trying to outwit Helmi, I noticed an Aberdeen newspaper clipping on the bulletin board just next to us. It announced to the world at large: "Helmi Juvonen was born in Butte, Montana, in 1903." There is just no keeping any secrets from the press, I concluded.

Helmi had enjoyed seeing Dee that afternoon. Helmi had only been teasing her a bit. There were other people, however, who came to see Helmi who immediately put her on guard when their questions became much too personal. Reporters wanted to know things that really were none of their business. After one such "interviewer" had left Helmi's room, Helmi turned to me. "Do you know how I get rid of snoopy people like him? I just tell each person something different. Then no one knows what to believe!" At first I didn't pay much attention to that advice. Later on I began to discover how effective a ploy it could be.

Helmi began to receive a great deal of attention from the media. She was regularly "rediscovered." She soon became just about the best-known "unrecognized" artist in the Pacific Northwest. I shuddered when I read one of the articles written about her. I prayed that no one had sent this particular article to her, because it talked in the most morbid way about her alleged past "mental disturbances." I phoned Helmi warily and sounded her out, mentioning that an article had come out. She was quick to get my drift and realize I was disturbed by what the article said about her. "Oh, Wes," she explained cheerfully, "when the newspapers write about you, sometimes they're going to say things about you that you like.

Other times, they're going to say things about you that you don't like at all. This sort of thing doesn't bother me. Don't worry about it! When we start to be in the public eye and written up in the newspapers, it's to be expected! Mark used to have a tantrum over some of the things they said about him in the papers!"

Even though Helmi often gave the impression of living in a world of her own, she was highly aware of the effect she had on people around her. She had her own sense of style and an unpredictable kind of showmanship that she used when she felt the occasion and moment were right. Toward the end of Helmi's life, she and I sat side by side on her metal hospital bed at the Oakhurst, thumbing through a picture book of cats and kittens. A few feet away from us, a young photographer was taking pictures of her. Helmi seemed oblivious to being photographed. Until, that is, she abruptly looked up from the cat pictures book and stared straight into the camera lens. "Wes and I are very theatrical!" she exclaimed. Journalists and friends invariably wanted to take pictures of Helmi. She obliged them all. Of the many photographs taken of Helmi in her older years, however, none is more characteristic and revealing than Mary Randlett's portrait of her sitting outdoors at Oakhurst, tenderly cradling a kitten in her lap.

Shortly before Helmi died in 1985, Joseph Newland, sculptor Mark Reeves, and I spent two afternoons with her at Oakhurst. We sat in her room, looking at picturebooks of cats and talking about old friends. We took her out for a short stroll on the lawn. Helmi was radiant. "Mama is coming any day now to take me home. I'm going to see my sister again!" she exclaimed. Helmi had already given most of her works to museums and friends. Her personal papers and sketch books had been formally transferred to the University of Washington Libraries. Her possessions now consisted only of what she felt she still needed—her books, her clothes, and a few art materials for sketching. Unencumbered, Helmi was now prepared for the greatest journey of her long life, and she awaited it eagerly.

It would be a drive of several hours back to Seattle from Elma. Joseph and Mark told Helmi how glad they were to see her again. Helmi hugged Joseph. "Take good care of Wes," she said. "From now on you're going to have to see to it for me that he gets his ten cups of coffee a day!" Sitting in a chair next to us, Mark had whittled a small wooden figure with his penknife while Joseph and I conversed with Helmi. Mark said goodbye to Helmi and joined Joseph in the hallway. I stayed behind for a moment to say goodbye to her.

The tenderness of Helmi's kiss on my cheek as I saw her for what was to be the last time startled me. It was so gentle and sad a kiss that as I started to leave I lingered in the doorway, looking back at her sitting on her sanitarium bed. I walked back to her. "Helmi, I liked that very much! Please— let's say goodbye again!"

When I called Helmi from Seattle several weeks later, the nurse brought her to the hallway telephone. "Is that you, Pumpkin?" she asked. "I have a cold I can't seem to shake off. But I'll be all right." Several days later, the nurse notified me that Helmi had been transferred for observation to the hospital in McCleary, several miles east of Elma. Another call followed the next day. Helmi had gone into a diabetic coma and died that morning. "Helmi was so cheerful this morning," the nurse told me on the phone. "She talked about her cats. She hoped someone was remembering to feed them. Her diabetic coma came on very suddenly. She died very peacefully."

ON OCTOBER 23, I went to Elma by Greyhound bus with Brent Goeres to attend Helmi's funeral. About sixty or seventy people, many of them quite elderly, came to pay their final respects. The pastor began to recount Helmi's life. Abruptly he looked up from his lectern notes and confronted us sternly. "This woman whom we loved so much had very little in the way of earthly goods. But she leaves a legacy to the world that can't be measured in mere dollars. She leaves us the gift of her art, which will endure long after you and I are forgotten. Ask yourselves as you sit here, ask yourselves, 'What have I given to the world? What do I leave behind when my time has come?'"

After Helmi's service, I wrote an account to my friend Ron Vize: "The funeral was very nice. The Daughters of the Eagles had gone to considerable trouble to prepare a banquet table of food across the street from the mortuary. After the funeral I had a few minutes alone with Helmi. I had gone to the service bearing some last messages and goodbyes for her from Joe Newland, Regina Hackett, and Deloris Tarzan Ament. I had tried to insulate myself against the stark fact that I'd never, ever be able to visit Helmi again."

AS A WARD OF THE STATE, Helmi was allowed to have only a minimum amount of money in her own name. She had a charge account at several of the stores in Elma. When she ran up her charges, or when her savings account was low, the bookkeeper at Oakhurst notified me and I sent a money order to Oakhurst. Helmi's brother-in-law, Darrell Asher, had prepaid a burial plot for her in Los Angeles. Darrell's deceased wife, Irene, was Helmi's sister. The day following Helmi's funeral, her remains were sent to Los Angeles, where she would be buried beside her mother and her sister at Forest Lawn cemetery.

Helmi Juvonen had a genius for making the most of any situation. During the many years she was confined at the Oakhurst Convalescent Center, her creative energies and sheer determination enabled her to make a life for herself in the midst of an environment that would have devastated a person of less imagination and intelligence. Though she received excellent care at Oakhurst and was even something of a local celebrity there, she still was subject to the routines of the institution. Even in her confinement as a ward of the state, however, she demonstrated a freedom of spirit and a practical resourcefulness that were an inspiration to the many young artists and friends who came to visit her. Helmi became for many of us a symbol of a life devoted purely to creativity in an infinite number of ways — both in her work and in the radiant optimism she brought to her life.

Guy Anderson

There is this great thing of walking out across the sod and
wading swamps where iris grow. Running the finger
through tall grass causing rills along the spine. Plunging
deep in secret places where the oceans pound. And running
in the wind that bruises pink the face. The seed, sometimes
called purusa, is in the mud bank. It was before the veins
of the hand or the coursing of rivers to the sea.
And it still dwells ever so mysteriously in the center.

— GUY ANDERSON, 1975

DURING THE CHRISTMAS HOLIDAYS of 1949 I went to Mark Tobey's house in the University district to deliver a Christmas present: the collected works of Edgar Allen Poe. I didn't know Tobey well enough then to know his taste in books. Poe seemed like a safe enough choice. Tobey unwrapped the present and responded politely, "Edgar Allen Poe! I haven't read him in years. Perhaps I should again. Thank you." Just then a strikingly handsome man came bounding down the stairs from the second floor and walked jauntily across the room toward us. "Have you met Guy Anderson?" Tobey asked me.

Tobey had earlier introduced me to Morris Graves. Now I was meeting another of those four painters whom *Life* magazine in 1953 would describe as the four "mystic painters" of the Pacific Northwest: Mark Tobey, Morris Graves, Guy Anderson, and Kenneth Callahan. Whatever notion I might have had of how a mystical painter should look was obliterated by meeting Guy Anderson. He looked more, I thought, like a dapper, suntanned movie star.

Though these painters were grouped as members of the same "school," I would learn how different they were from one another—especially Mark Tobey and Guy Anderson.

Tobey had a militantly competitive streak, notably so when other painters were receiving more recognition than he. He was insistent, too, on being credited for any influence he might have had on any other painter. He craved constant recognition. Ironically, when finally he did become famous, he complained that he had lost his privacy, that he was surrounded by opportunists. He could always find some reason or another for complaining.

Guy Anderson liked recognition, too. But only in small

Guy Anderson, La Conner, Washington, August 1981
(Photograph by Paul Dahlquist)

doses. He was glad when enough of his work sold that he didn't have to worry about money. He seemed indifferent to the possibility of becoming "one of the top bananas," his way of describing "the big names" in the current marketplace. He seemed to know exactly what he needed. As long as he had enough to get by on and to keep painting, that's what mattered most to him. He sidestepped the kinds of public attention that would have only complicated his life. Painter William Cumming described him aptly: "I have never known Guy to raise his voice in argument, never known him to express spiteful or angry feelings. His warmth is impersonal and almost detached, imposing no emotional obligation on his friends."

GUY ANDERSON WAS BORN IN EDMONDS, Washington, on November 20, 1906. His father, Irving Anderson, ran a small carpentry business, played the clarinet, and was a Socialist. Both his parents loved art and music. They encouraged Guy to take piano lessons—which he did for six years—and to become an artist. They also encouraged him and his two sisters to think for themselves. With such a supportive and liberal family background, it is not surprising that he became an artist with an independent streak—both in his art and in how he conducted his life.

As a young boy, he was taken by his parents to the natural history museum on the University of Washington campus to see the birds' nests, rare minerals, exotic sea shells, pressed plants, mummies, and especially the great collections of Pacific Northwest Native American art. The totems and wooden carvings by the Haida, Kwakiutl, Nootka, and other northern tribes left a lasting impression on him.

After graduating from Edmonds High School, he enrolled at Eustace Paul Ziegler's art school in downtown Seattle. A well-known and fashionable painter of the Alaskan and Northwest landscape, Ziegler had studied art at Yale and could provide his students with a solid background in life drawing, still life, portraiture, and landscape painting.

In 1929 Morris Graves, who was nineteen at the time, saw several of Anderson's paintings in an exhibition in Seattle and sought him out in his Edmonds studio. Anderson and Graves subsequently became close friends and often shared the same studio. During 1934 and 1935 they traveled through Oregon and California in a pickup truck, using it as both a studio and a home. When they reached Los Angeles, Anderson traveled on alone to Texas and into northern Mexico.

The technical training Anderson had earlier received from Ziegler enabled him to try his hand at teaching. During the 1950s he taught art briefly at the Helen Bush School in Seattle. Teaching, he soon discovered, was not for him.

As Anderson approached middle age he needed to simplify his life and concentrate on his painting. His "career" (if he ever did have one) would have to fend for itself. In 1955 he moved to La Conner, a small fishing village at the mouth of the Skagit River, some forty-five miles north of Seattle. For several years he rented a one-storey house at the edge of town. It was nestled against the side of a small hill and was separated from the distant road by a beet patch. Visitors had to walk through property owner Axel Jensen's back yard and down a forest trail to reach Anderson's cabin. He lived frugally. He planted a garden, and did most of his own cooking. He spent the mornings and afternoons painting.

On the stone ledge just above his house was a secluded spot where he sketched his models or sunbathed during the summer. When I brought friends to meet him, I had to make sure he knew we were coming.

In the evening Guy walked into town to socialize and play shuffleboard at the La Conner Tavern. He greeted everyone in the tavern or in the street with the same cordiality. I noticed how adept he was at sidestepping heated debates and not taking sides unnecessarily. He avoided confrontations of any sort. As we walked back to his cabin one night, Guy stopped on the road and turned to me. "You may be wondering to yourself why I spend so much time with all these people. I do like and enjoy them. Besides, they don't invade the part of me that paints, the way so many people in Seattle do," he explained.

Some of the works Guy painted in La Conner during the 1960s were inspired by his childhood memories of the northern tribal art he had seen at the campus museum. These include *Guardians of the Symbol* (1963), *Burial in Winter* (1965), *Northern Birth* (1967), and *Corner of the Earth* (1968). These paintings are among his most powerful and moving works. It was rare for me to see any "Alaskan" paintings that weren't illustrational and insipid when compared with the authentic Pacific Northwest Native American art. Sydney Lawrence and the other painters of the Alaskan scene were traditional in their approach. Mark Tobey had painted a few pictures based on Native American totemic art, but he was dissatisfied with them. "It's never like the real thing," he said.

I wondered about these northern paintings of Guy's. They had a rare depth and authenticity about them. One evening in July 1996, while visiting him in La Conner, I asked him if he had spent any time in Alaska.

"Yes, I was in Alaska for at least two months while I was studying with Eustace Ziegler. It was near the North Pole. I was pretty much alone much of the time. I didn't have any trouble. It wasn't cold at all. The animals would swim the rivers to come over to look at us. From the way they looked at us, you knew they had never seen humans before."

I wrote this down in my notebook as he spoke, and read it back to him.

"Yes, that's right. That's just the way it was!"

ALTHOUGH GUY LIVED IN LA CONNER, his paintings were regularly exhibited in Seattle. Young painters were interested in his work because it was original and entirely apart from all the current trends and "isms" going the rounds in Seattle and elsewhere. Some of these young painters occasionally asked me to arrange for them to meet the "great artist," "the mystical master," and the "living legend."

One afternoon I arrived at Guy's door in La Conner accompanied by an especially reverential type of young painter. How could I warn this kid to be ready for just about anything?

I knocked on the door. A moment later, the door opened a little bit and a scowling face peered out at us. The door opened wide. The young painter and I were confronted by what appeared to be the maid. It wasn't the maid at all. It was Guy wearing a shaggy black wig and a maid's uniform.

"What do you want, anyway?" demanded the irate servant.

Solemnly I announced: "This young painter and I would like very much to meet Guy Anderson, the great master."

"And what gives you the idea Mr. Anderson would have

any time for the likes of you?" snapped this fearsome guardian of Guy Anderson's privacy, slamming the door right in our faces.

The young painter was bewildered. "What the hell is going on?" he asked me.

The door opened again. Guy Anderson, this time without the grotesque wig and disheveled maid's uniform, welcomed us in. "Oh, that terrible maid!" he exclaimed. "I've just fired her and sent her packing. I wondered why I hadn't seen anyone in days. She was scaring everybody off. Please come in. I'm so glad to have some company!"

By now the young painter was thoroughly disoriented. Was this Guy Anderson, the painter. Or was this some madcap rerun of a Marx Brothers movie?

WHEN HE CAME TO SEATTLE for the opening of an exhibition of his works, Guy's idea of celebrating was to invite a number of his relatively impoverished young artist and poet friends out for dinner after the gallery preview. As we all sat around the table at Nikko's Japanese restaurant in the International District, Guy announced to us, "Have anything you want. It's on me — and the sky's the limit!" While many other local painters worked diligently at expanding their social networks and advancing their professional careers, appearing at all the important previews and buttering up prospective patrons, Guy would have none of that.

Even when he didn't have all that much money, Guy would always help out a young painter or an old friend who had fallen on bad times. My painting sales were few and far between, and I didn't have any dependable source of income. My curatorship in paleontology at the Burke Museum at the

University of Washington had many benefits, but a salary was not one of them. When Guy realized this, he began to send me checks, month after month, year after year. He assured me he could readily afford it. "Tobey helped me out when I needed it. Now that my paintings are selling pretty well, it's my turn to help you out," he explained.

Guy's living room and adjoining studio were always piled high with art books. On the grand piano were stacks of sheet music, bouquets of dried flowers from the nearby fields, polished pieces of petrified wood, beach agates, rusted pieces of metal, and ceramics by potter friends. One way or another, many of these objects eventually found their way into his works. The texture of the sky in one of his paintings looked very much like that of the pale blue agate from Brazil on his writing table. The earth in another painting had the same color as the rusted tin can he had found on the road to town the previous year. Even his most figurative paintings had the feeling of landscapes.

Poet Elizabeth Bishop visited Guy in La Conner in 1966. She noticed that several of the landscapes in his studio contained the local cows, especially a large painting entitled *Sacred Pasture*. She liked how Guy painted out of his immediate environment. By contrast, to her distress, some of her poetry students were writing "haikus" and poems filled with bamboo, goldfish, and all the trappings of Asian art and poetry. Elizabeth urged them to write about the objects that were part of their own daily lives. She said to me later, "I noticed today that Guy Anderson has several cows in his paintings. I haven't written any poetry while I've been in Seattle. But if I were to, I just might take a cue from Mr. Anderson and put a cow or two in my poem."

During the early 1980s, sculptor Mark Reeves and I often drove to Princeton, British Columbia, to collect fossils. On our way back to Seattle we stopped at Guy's studio to show him our finds. We spread them out on his patio table.

"Take what you want, Guy. Any of it. Whatever you want," we told him. Guy was intrigued by these fifty-million-year-old fossil leaves. Their oxidized colors of orange, brown, red, and black, their mottled textures, and their irregular shapes reminded him of ancient Japanese and Chinese ceramic shards.

"We're so locked into the rectilinear forms that we don't realize how interesting these irregularly shaped forms can be. I should study these fossils carefully," he said.

GUY ANDERSON COULD APPEAR at first to be unguardedly approachable, amiable, and articulate. He was, however, so private a person that one might have known him for some fifty years, as I did, and still only have begun to know him. He was not by nature secretive or evasive. His politeness and decorum were genuine. His generosity had no hidden agendas.

Sometime during the mid-1980s, after I had already known him for some thirty years, our friendship deepened. I began to turn to him more and more for advice, often of the most personal kind. There were very few older close friends left now to whom I could go when I needed perspective. As I confided more and more in him, I discovered in him an extraordinary depth and wisdom.

As an artist and human being, Guy Anderson was an inspiration. Young painters sought him out, and he quickly became a role model for many of them, myself included. He had managed to sidestep so many of the incessant trivialities and distractions of an ordinary life. As he grew old, he seemed to accept his increasing infirmities with such good nature. He never for a moment acted as if he felt sorry for himself, nor did he express regrets of any kind. So many artists may create memorable, lasting works, but as human beings they may seem petty and mean-spirited. Guy Anderson embodied for me a true nobility of spirit.

Morris Graves:
An Evening in Loleta

DURING THE SUMMER of 1949, Mark Tobey invited me to a party at his house in the University District. Pehr Hallsten, his companion, greeted me at the door and introduced me to some of the guests, telling them I was a composer.

"Wes is teaching Mark how to compose music!" Pehr told the guests.

Considering that I was nineteen at the time and Mark Tobey was sixty, the idea of my being his music composition teacher seemed at the least improbable, even though it happened to be true. Our mutual teacher, Lockrem Johnson, was away for the summer, so I was pinch-hitting as Tobey's music teacher.

I noticed a man standing alone across the room. He was observing everything that went on without participating in any of it. Without his doing or saying anything, his very presence dominated the room. To say he was handsome would be an understatement.

"Have you met Morris Graves yet?" a voice behind me asked. It was Tobey, carrying a tray of coffee cups and cookies.

"No, I haven't, and I would very much like to," I answered.

Tobey introduced me to Graves, who asked me about the music I wrote. We conversed for only a few minutes. Several of his admirers arrived at the party, spotted him, and descended upon him.

I HAD SEEN several of Morris Graves's paintings at the Henry Art Gallery the previous week: *Snake and Moon, In the Air, Asian Bloom,* and *Sea, Fish, and Constellation.* I had also seen his famous *Little Known Bird of the Inner Eye* reproduced in several books on modern painting during the late 1940s. After meeting him, I went to the Seattle Art Museum to look at more of his paintings. The uniquely personal nature of these works was a compelling experience for me. I was struck by their expressive range. Although they depicted birds and animals, and rarely ever any human beings, they conveyed many qualities of human feeling—intimate experiences with which I could instantly identify. *In the Air* depicted two luminous birds meeting above the earth, the very experience of being in love, of being lovers. *Asian Bloom,* with its exploding, shimmering halo of white light, was as tender and beautiful as the loveliest music. His *Rising Moon* paintings were dialogues between human solitude and the mysteries of the night.

The sullen ferocity of some of his birds. The delicacy

and frailty of others. The shore birds moving in unison with the beach tides, like the movements of crowds in city streets, obeying the traffic lights and social trends.

I was amazed by how much of the "human condition" Morris Graves conveyed while staying entirely within the realm of nature. The Henry Art Gallery captions described Morris Graves's paintings as "mystical" and "spiritual." Nonetheless, I found some of them to be very sensual, even erotic —the entwined snakes especially so. His paintings spoke of asceticism and ecstasy; they were both spiritual and earthly. My own notion of religious spirituality was bleaker, more barrenly Nordic—with seemingly unresolvable conflicts between spirit and flesh. I was startled by the deep unities of human experience I sensed in Graves's paintings—experiences which in my own life might have seemed contradictory or fragmented. His paintings were not only beautiful aesthetic objects; they were, for me, paths to other kinds of personal knowledge and living.

AS I GOT TO KNOW him better, Morris struck me as being very much like his paintings—at times disarmingly tender, even vulnerable; at times intensely but obliquely intimate; and at other times reserved, remote, abruptly cool. His charisma could be mesmerizing and a little frightening. I felt overwhelmed by him—intrigued, but wary.

During October 1950, I moved into a small room at the Kennedy Building on University Way. Pehr Hallsten had a

Morris Graves and his dog, Edith, in Woodway Park, August 1949.
Graves had several dogs during these years, each consecutively
named Edith (Photograph by Mary Randlett)

room on the second floor, facing University Way, where he read during the afternoons while Mark Tobey was painting in his studio down the street. Helmi Juvonen would visit Pehr during the afternoons. She sat in the corner, drawing while Pehr read.

Painter Ward Corley, a close friend of Morris's, lived on the floor below me. Ward suggested that he and I exchange rooms. By trading rooms with him, I acquired introductions to some of his artist friends — Richard Gilkey, Jan Thompson, and Jack Stangl. When they came looking for him I had to explain that Ward now lived upstairs.

Helmi dropped by regularly. Tobey and Pehr left notes on my door: "We are out for an evening stroll. Sorry to miss you." Poet Richard Selig would show up at midnight or later. He had just written a new poem. My professors wondered why I looked so bleary when I showed up in the mornings for music theory class.

A KNOCK CAME on my door one evening. Standing in the dimly lit hallway was Morris.

"You're not Ward. Didn't I just meet you at Tobey's party?" he asked.

I invited him in. My room's furnishings consisted of a small bed, an upright piano, and a small table. The glare of the bare light bulb on the ceiling was merciless. Morris winced, shielded his eyes, and made himself at home on my cotlike bed.

"Why don't you play something for me? One of your own compositions," he suggested.

I had just finished composing a short piece for piano, an impressionistic sort of music, which I played for him. When

I finished, Morris rose from the bed, put on his coat, thanked me somewhat formally, and disappeared into the night.

DURING THE CHRISTMAS HOLIDAY of 1960, I painted some little pictures, landscapes. I didn't exactly "paint" them. Instead, I used drug-store crayolas and an improvised kind of encaustic technique. For heat, I used cigarette matches. After a long night of "painting" with crayon wax and burning matches, the other tenants in the rooming house where I lived usually started to complain about the smoke fumes drifting down the hallways.

That same holiday, Morris arrived in Seattle for a brief visit. He was staying at the Meany Hotel. When he invited me to drop by his room, I arrived with several small paintings to show him. He looked at them for what seemed an eternity.

"You don't have to be concerned with 'finding' yourself. You already have. These paintings are very much your own. I can see how they come out of things that have meaning for you—the sky, the beaches, the desert . . . those polished stones you showed me, the ones that look like landscapes and seascapes," he said.

He looked at the paintings again.

"I have very good hearing, better than most people have. I can 'hear' these paintings of yours quite clearly. But other people don't always have hearing as good as mine. I would suggest that when you paint you turn up the volume a little more."

Tobey insisted that it took years and years of hard work before a genuine personality could emerge in a painter. Morris was telling me that I had already found my own "voice," in an embryonic form. Now, he added, it needed to be "amplified" and intensified, so that others could "hear" and enjoy it too.

I sometimes showed the same paintings to both Tobey and Morris. The pale blue sky in one seascape was a flat, unmodulated blue. Tobey looked at it first: "You should look at Corot's skies. They have very subtle changes of color in them. Your sky is too uniform. It needs a lot of reworking. A picture plane should be a journey. Things should happen along the way when the eye travels across it, just as they do when we travel somewhere. When my eye moves across your sky, nothing happens! I don't *go* anywhere. You haven't nuanced and activated your sky." Tobey had been, as usual, very analytical in explaining to me why this painting did not satisfy him.

Morris came into my room several days later. He went over to the same painting upon which Tobey had just commented. He studied it: "It's quite lovely, of course. But I keep waiting for a bird to fly across that sky! I keep waiting for something more to happen!"

Morris had made virtually the same point as Tobey. But Morris, unlike Tobey, could be exact without being theoretical and didactic.

WHEN MORRIS NEXT VISITED my room I had framed and hung a painting entitled *Sage County*. I was so proud of how accurately I had depicted sagebrush.

Morris studied the painting: "That's quite beautiful. That certainly looks like sagebrush. But I like much better those paintings of yours that suggest things rather than resemble them so closely as this. The minute I look at this painting, I say to myself, 'That's sage brush.' As soon as I can name it, the mystery of the painting ceases to exist for me."

Commenting finally on the painting's frame, he added, "That must be a good frame. I didn't even notice it until just now."

I continued to paint, and I began to exhibit a few paintings here and there. When Morris returned to Seattle several years later I visited him again at the Meany Hotel. He asked how the painting was going.

"I'm surprised at how easy it seems for me to paint. But I'm starting to worry that a time may come when the painting just doesn't flow the way it does now," I answered.

Morris shot me a disturbed look. He went to the hotel window and looked out at the city and the distant Olympic Mountains. With carefully measured words, he responded: "First of all, you haven't painted any paintings."

I was startled. What did he mean by that?

"No, you haven't *painted* any paintings. What I mean is that you have allowed nature to come through in your work. Your ego hasn't intruded into these works of yours. But if you start thinking that you 'painted' these pictures, then you may be in trouble!" he said.

Morris's remarks to me sounded quite similar to what Tobey's mentor, Mr. Takesaki, had told Tobey: "Get yourself out of the way when you paint!"

SEVERAL YEARS LATER, I visited Morris at the Pletscheff mansion on Capitol Hill while he was staying there. We sat in the living room, drinking coffee.

"I have some new paintings in the next room. Perhaps you'd like to see them," Morris announced.

"Of course, I would!" I said, starting to rise from my chair.

Morris changed his mind. "No, I don't think I should

show them to you after all. They're not all that good, and I don't want to disappoint you. Unless I was sure you were going to be swept off your feet by them I would hesitate to show them to you. I don't want to show you anything that I already know will probably disappoint you, even though I know you would be very kind about it."

DURING THE MID-1960S, writer Hiroaki Sato visited Seattle for a few days. He was staying at the Meany Hotel when I went to visit him. I asked Hiroaki what bothered him most when he visited the United States.

"When I first got here, people expected me to have an opinion about *everything*. Did I like this? Did I dislike that? Most of the time I was just enjoying looking at things. I didn't have any opinions to offer these people," he answered. As an afterthought, he added, "I don't think we Japanese have solved this problem either—this always having to say one thing is better than another, as if they should always be compared. But I think we're more flexible about it than you Westerners seem to be."

MORRIS GRAVES began to ask me questions for which I had no satisfactory answers. We had, for instance, just visited an exhibition of Morris Louis's recent paintings, a series entitled *Veils*. We left the Seattle Center's Modern Art Pavilion and walked over to a bench beside a group of tall cypress trees. It was a lovely summer afternoon. The sky was a cloudless blue. A small breeze cooled the air. We sat looking at the cypress trees towering above us.

"Which do you prefer, Wes, those paintings back there, or these trees?" Morris asked me.

"Do I really have to chose between them? Can't I enjoy both?" I responded.

I thought a bit more about it.

"When it comes down to it, I'd really prefer to sit under these trees *after* looking at those paintings. I wouldn't want to look at *them* after having sat here under those trees. And on such a lovely afternoon as this!" I added.

THE FOLLOWING YEAR, Morris returned to Seattle after a visit to Kyoto. A monastery abbot there had shown him the famed scroll entitled *Seven Persimmons*, one of the greatest treasures in the entire history of Japanese art.

"The abbot put a question to me: Which is more important, this scroll or a bowl of rice? How would you have answered him?" Morris asked me.

"I would have eaten the scroll right there and then," I replied.

Morris gave me a most odd look.

DURING THE 1960S Morris settled in northern California, near the town of Loleta, several miles south of Eureka. His house was beside a small lake, in a forest of old-growth redwood trees. His visits to Seattle became less frequent. We lost touch with each other for as much as a year or two at a time. I had some of the most fond and endearing memories of him. I also had memories that were anything but endearing. It was difficult for me to resolve in myself the various sides of Morris I had known. Nevertheless, I wanted very much to see him again.

During the summer of 1969, young painter Joseph Goldberg and I borrowed a car and filled it up with camping gear, sleeping bags, and rockhounding tools. After a week in the Oregon desert and a drive through the California coastal redwood forests, we stopped at Eureka for dinner around five o'clock in the evening. I phoned Morris in Loleta to tell him Joe and I were passing through town on our way to southern California.

"Can you come out to the lake for a drink? You should remember how to get here. You've been here before. Could you be here by eight? I can see you for an hour, but no more," he said.

Morris had said he could see us for only an hour, no more. Not wanting to waste a single minute of such a visit, Joe and I would have to see to it that we were at his door at precisely eight o'clock. It took a bit of doing. We synchronized our wrist watches and set out for Morris's house. From Loleta we turned off the highway onto a dirt road. There was a gate to be opened, then closed. We drove past a farmhouse. There was another gate to be opened and closed. Finally we reached the narrow dirt road that led into the redwood forest and eventually to Morris's house.

We arrived at his house at least twenty minutes early, despite fearing we might be late. We sat in the car, smoking cigarettes, watching the clock hands move slowly toward eight o'clock. A few moments before the stroke of eight, we walked up to Morris's door, watching the clock's second hand. Precisely at the hour, we knocked on the door. The door promptly opened and Morris greeted us, "How nice to see you again! Won't you come in."

He quickly showed us a bit of his house, a glimpse down a hallway, a peek into another room.

"My studio is down there," Morris said, pointing down another hall, as he led us into the living room.

Morris looked much the same as I had remembered him. He was sixty years old now, but time had neither stooped nor visibly aged him. He was as physically imposing as ever. His eyes, in a single sharp and guarded glance, could still size up a person or a situation.

"Will you have a drink? Will whiskey be all right? I haven't been to town for a while, so I can't offer you much of a choice," he explained.

Morris left the room and returned a few minutes later with our drinks. We settled into some large cushions on the floor by the fireplace.

"Before we start talking, I'll have to remind you to leave by nine o'clock. I have a very full day ahead tomorrow," he said.

Morris pointed out the window at the fading light on the lake beside his house. "Isn't it beautiful here, especially in the evening!" he said.

He turned to Joe, "Wes came here to stay with me several years ago. But I think he became bored with all this beauty and silence. I never understood why he left so abruptly. He seemed to want to get back to his University District in Seattle, and I can't stand being there anymore."

Even though Morris was in a good mood, the conversation that evening took some strange twists and turns.

"Tell me, Joseph, how do you feel about death?" Morris asked Joe unexpectedly.

"I don't know how I feel about death, Mr. Graves. But when I do die, I'll try to let you know then," Joe answered.

Somewhat seriously, Morris said, "I find the prospect of

actual physical pain far more disturbing than the abstract thought of death and dying."

I could pretty well follow that. It reminded me of the old adage that a philosopher can handle just about anything but a toothache.

Morris brought us another drink. I glanced at my wristwatch and noticed that nine o'clock was approaching. Should I remind Morris of this, I wondered? He seemed to be enjoying himself, so I said nothing. Abruptly, he changed the subject. "Wes, you used to write me such beautiful little letters, ones that I've cherished. Why, I still carry your last one in me old spectacle case, next to me old heart. I'll go get it now, in case you don't believe me," he said.

He was right. I had indeed written many letters to him over the years, but his responses were few and far between. I never quite knew how he regarded some of the things I wrote him, including my fumbling expressions of admiration and guarded affection.

He left the room and returned moments later with his spectacle case, and in it, beneath his eyeglasses was a folded note. "You see, here it is," he said, handing the note to me. I remembered this note very well. Morris and I had attended a dinner party in Seattle. He had shocked the august group of dinner guests by proposing that money intended to be spent for public art at the airport be spent instead on trying to legalize marijuana. Several of the dinner guests were horrified by Morris's speech. I had scrawled this affectionate note to him quickly and slipped it to him under the dinner table. Morris, the master of the unexpected, had been in top form that evening.

He had indeed saved my note. I was surprised and very pleased.

"But you don't write notes like this to me anymore," he said. "I guess I'm no longer worthy of your affections. Maybe you'll say you don't write to me anymore because I don't always answer your letters. But if you really loved me, you wouldn't expect an answer. You'd continue to write me anyway. Ah, pity! I shall try to go on. Somehow!"

Was he just pulling my leg, just putting me on? With Morris, one never knew.

By now it was already well past nine o'clock. Our visit was winding down. It would be a long drive to the next campground.

Morris turned to Joe. "I will tell you something about Wes," he said. "I have known him for a very long time. He is one of the kindest, most thoughtful, most sensitive of people. He would not deliberately hurt anyone."

Looking intently at me, Morris continued, "But I will tell you something else about Wes. Should the day ever come when he chooses to be cruel, God spare us all!"

Several years earlier Morris had told a mutual friend, Bob Mony, "Wes may seem vulnerable, but beneath his surface he is like steel!"

Remarks such as these, especially coming from Morris, sobered and confused me. Had he detected something in me that, even had I recognized it, I would have had trouble accepting? Any personal observations by Morris were not to be taken lightly, or easily brushed aside. He had an uncanny gift for seeing past peoples' facades and masks, and their self-deceptions.

I tried to change the subject quickly. "Morris, if you could have a complaint, only one complaint, about anything at all, what would that be?" I asked him.

"My complaint would be," he answered, "that I am so confined by the form into which I was born."

MY COMPLAINT, when I attempt to write about this great artist, this complex and marvelous man, is that I too am confined — confined by my inability even to begin to do him admiring justice. His paintings and drawings stand apart among the finest and most original done in our time, not only for their superlative aesthetic beauty but also for the depth of their intuitive insight into the mysterious and finally solitary journey of living itself.

Zoe Dusanne: Impresario
of the "Northwest School"

HOW DID THE NOTION of a "Northwest School" of mystical painters arise in the first place? I would credit Seattle art collector and dealer Zoe Dusanne not only with having the idea but with having the flair and contacts with which to promote it. In 1952 Dusanne suggested to a friend on the staff of *Life* magazine that there were several remarkable painters in this area—Mark Tobey, Morris Graves, Guy Anderson, and Kenneth Callahan—whose personalities and work could make a very interesting story. She described them as solitary, "mystical" painters living and working in the far reaches of the Pacific Northwest.

The following year, *Life* magazine published an article entitled "Mystic Painters of the Northwest." None of us then could have predicted that a single article in a popular national magazine would play such an influential role in shaping popular and scholarly perceptions of the painting scene in the Pacific Northwest. This magazine story, for better or worse, took Zoe Dusanne's label and effectively assured a place in local art history for Tobey, Graves, Anderson, and Callahan. Such is the power of the press.

I FIRST MET ZOE DUSANNE, "creator" of the "Northwest School," at a small dinner party given by a mutual friend, Eunice Clise. Eunice and I were fellow students in Theodore Roethke's verse-writing class. Zoe was definitely the center of attention that evening. The rest of us, her young admirers, listened silently to her colorful and often ribald accounts of all the famous painters she had known. No one else could get a word in, even edgewise. Zoe did not take kindly to being interrupted, and once she got going, there was no stopping her. The sheer number of her stories began to daze the other dinner guests. Exhausted by this seemingly endless flow of anecdotes, I turned to painter Bob West and said as quietly as I could, "Good God, there's no end to this! Who *didn't* she know? Next I suppose she'll name-drop the Pope!"

Zoe's hearing was sharper than I realized. "I heard that, young man," she said, smiling. "Thank you for reminding me. As a matter of fact, I did meet the Pope once. It was in New York, before he became Pope. He was a cardinal then. I even shook hands with him through a car window." I turned to Bob in resignation. Zoe always had the last word.

ZOE WORE A PURPLE WIG. In the early 1950s, that was daring. It follows that the stories about her were never humdrum. She confided to me that she was born in Guadalajara and was descended from Jean Lafitte, the French pirate. One

Wes Wehr and Zoe Dusanne in her apartment near the Seattle
Center, 1966. Reflected in the mirror are paintings by Paul Klee,
Marcel Duchamp, Piet Mondrian, and Mark Tobey
(Photograph by Mary Randlett)

rumor, among many, claimed she had been the madame in a notorious New Orleans brothel. Another story hinted that she was descended from an Inca princess. Be that as it may, Zoe and her daughter Theodosia bore the names of Byzantine empresses. None of us, however, really knew all that much about her. Zoe was so colorful that we would have believed anything about her past, except that it had been ordinary.

During the early 1950s Mark Tobey exhibited his works at Zoe's gallery on Lakeview Boulevard. The gallery space was in Zoe's living room, in a contemporary ranch-style house with a view of Lake Union. In the adjoining rooms Zoe hung works from her private collection — paintings by Paul Klee, Piet Mondrian, Wassily Kandinsky, Jean Arp, Stuart Davis, John Graham, Robert and Sonia Delaunay, Ben Nicholson, Lyonel Feininger, Claire Falkenstein, Charmion von Wiegand, and Mark Tobey, among others. Each painting in her collection had its own story of how she had acquired it, often from the artist's studio. She told me stories about the years when she lived and worked in New York during the 1940s. She would pinch and scrape to put aside enough money to buy paintings — walking to work rather than taking the subway, skipping lunch, doing without.

Zoe brought a rich and uniquely personal background to our Seattle cultural scene. She introduced us to the anecdotal side of painters whom many of us had known only through art books, or reproductions, or sometimes an original work. Zoe's advice was always practical. She told us that if ever we saw a good painting we couldn't afford, we should immediately put some money down on it, adding, "That's how I bought my Mondrian. I put ten dollars down on it. I was also going to buy one of Pete's last paintings from him. I wanted to make a deposit on it, but he said I didn't need to. He died just after that, so I lost out on owning a great Mondrian painting."

"Pete" Mondrian? Zoe must have noticed my raising an eyebrow at such implied familiarity with Mondrian. "I always called him 'Pete.' He liked it when I did," she explained.

One story inevitably led to another, and then another. "That reminds me," she continued. "When I went to Pete's studio in Manhattan, I noticed everything was spotlessly white. The only thing that wasn't white was his painting smock. It was black. I asked him about that. He had a practical explanation: a black smock didn't show the paint smudges so much."

NONE OF US had the faintest idea how old Zoe was, and she was not about to give us a clue. Age was *not* going to dim her luster. Even when she appeared in public during her final years she was usually the center of attention. If anyone told her how great she looked that evening, Zoe always had the same response, "Thank you very much. But as my mother used to say: A little powder and a little paint can make a gal look like what she ain't!"

As a dealer Zoe introduced the works of many important artists, not only to the Northwest but nationally as well. She was the first American dealer to exhibit Sam Francis's watercolors and to bring the paintings of French writer and artist Henri Michaux to this country. She also held the first American exhibition of works by the young Japanese artist Yayoi Kusama, who came to Seattle from Japan in 1957 for the exhibition. Kusama next went on to New York, where she created a furor of publicity and notoriety with her "happenings." In the intervening forty years, Kusama's reputation in Japan and New York has reached mythic proportions. She has recently had large exhibitions at the Museum of Modern Art in New York and at the Los Angeles County Museum of Art.

When I arrived at Zoe's gallery during Kusama's 1957 show, Zoe introduced me to Miss Kusama. At first impression, Kusama was doll-like, even delicate. I quickly realized she was a sheer terror as she launched into a tirade about the need for social liberation and free love in the modern world.

When Miss Kusama found out that I knew Mark Tobey, she asked me to arrange a personal meeting with him. Actually, she didn't so much make a request as she issued an executive order. Her reason for wanting to meet Tobey was startling and impressive in its brazen self-confidence. She announced to Zoe and me: "In Europe there is Picasso. In America there is Tobey. In Japan there is Yayoi. I wish to meet Mr. Tobey. Will you please arrange this!"

Zoe was greatly amused. "You're on your own this time," she whispered to me.

The next day I went to Tobey's house in the University District and relayed to him Kusama's pronouncement. He had no interest in meeting her. "Please tell Miss Kusama that Tobey does not wish to meet Yayoi!"

ZOE DUSANNE'S PREVIEW openings were well attended because the works she exhibited were invariably of high quality. But I remember one opening for a different reason. Zoe owned a large Siamese cat—Nebi—named for Nebuchadnezzar, the Chaldean King of Babylon. At this particular opening, a prominent art collector complained to Zoe that, although she needed to use the bathroom, it was already occupied—by a cat! Nebi sat regally on the toilet seat, facing the open door. She was not about to relinquish her place to anyone. Clearly she liked to perch on the toilet seat because it gave her such a good look at the people attending the preview.

THE FOUNDER AND DIRECTOR of the Seattle Art Museum, Richard E. Fuller, purchased over thirty paintings from the Dusanne gallery which he presented to the Seattle Art Museum. These works included Marcel Duchamp's *Discs Bearing Spirals*, Fernand Leger's *Mechanique No. 2*, and Francis Picabia's *Barcelone*. Zoe's own donations to the Seattle Art Museum and the Henry Art Gallery included works by Franz Marc, Joseph Stella, John Franklin Koenig, and Bernard Schultze. Interior designer Jean Jongeward bought from Zoe two of the best paintings I've ever seen for sale in a Seattle gallery—a large 1950s oil by Sam Francis, and an unsurpassingly beautiful early landscape by Zoran Music.

Zoe was in Europe during the summer of 1953. She talked to many of her European art critic and painter friends about Mark Tobey's work. She even traded a major 1942 Tobey white-writing painting, *The Meeting*, to French art critic Michel Tapie in exchange for a large oil by Picabia. "I thought it would do Mark more good to have that important work of his in Paris than in my house in Seattle," Zoe explained to me.

When Zoe returned from Europe that autumn, however, she was devastated to learn that Tobey, without telling her, had financed the opening of a new gallery in the University District. It would be run by Tobey's French teacher, Otto Seligman. This meant, Zoe realized, that she no longer represented Tobey in Seattle. To make matters even worse, several of her best artists — Guy Anderson, Pat Nicolson, and Windsor Utley — also left her gallery, going with Tobey to Seligman. Tobey never attempted to offer any explanation or excuse for doing such a thing to Zoe. She was stunned and hurt by Tobey's not only leaving her gallery but financing a rival gallery.

During the late 1950s, Zoe was confronted by even more bad news. The new freeway would cut right through the site of her house on Lakeview Boulevard. But Zoe was unsinkable. She realized there was no point to living in the past and letting these setbacks do her in. She relocated her gallery in a large apartment on Broadway Avenue on Capitol Hill. It didn't have the same elegance and the great view of Lake Union, but she managed to turn the space into an attractive gallery. And even though her adjoining living area was small, it was comfortable. She exhibited works by Sam Francis, Henri Michaux, Claire Falkenstein, S. W. Hayter, George Mathieu, Sonia Delaunay, Echaurren Matta, and other internationally known artists, and by such Northwest artists as Paul Horiuchi, Paul Dahlquist, Neil Meitzler, John Franklin Koenig, and Robert West.

I continued to visit both Zoe Dusanne and Otto Seligman, although neither of them liked this a single bit. Otto accused me of being a spy for Zoe, and Zoe always asked me how Otto's business was doing. She despised him and was bitter that he became Tobey's dealer just as Tobey was about to become world famous and successful, winning first prize in painting at the Venice Biennale, and having a retrospective exhibition at the Musee des Arts Decorativs at the

Louvre in Paris. It was Otto who would now reap the benefits of Zoe's hard work on Tobey's behalf. To make matters worse, Otto, taking advantage of Tobey's contacts, began to acquire for his gallery some of the other artists Zoe had known as friends and had represented. Even though I saw a good deal of Otto and had something of a friendship with him, I felt he was heartless in his indifference to Zoe's situation.

Many years went by. Mark rarely mentioned Zoe, who still felt deeply hurt by the rupturing of her friendship with him. On the evening of August 13, 1964, a gala crowd assembled at the Seattle Center Opera House for the formal unveiling of Mark Tobey's large mural, *Journey of an Opera Star*. I sat next to Zoe on the mezzanine that evening, watching Tobey several yards away, surrounded by people. Finally Zoe turned to me and said, "This has gone on long enough. Neither Mark nor I has much time left. There's no time left for pride." With that Zoe stood up and walked over to Mark, extending her hand to him. They looked into each other's probing eyes, hesitated, and embraced. Zoe came back to where I sat. "I'm so glad we've finally made up," she said. "I didn't want to die without making up with Mark."

A week later Zoe and Theodosia invited Tobey, his secretary Mark Ritter, and me to dinner at the apartment they shared near the Seattle Center. All the past ugliness seemed forgotten. Tobey and Zoe swapped stories about old friends. In Zoe's bedroom, Tobey saw a painting by Pehr, an especially nice one. Tobey told Zoe how much he had always liked that particular painting. "Here, I want you to have it," said Zoe, taking it off the wall and presenting it to Tobey. When the two Marks and I took a cab back to the Wilsonian

Hotel that night, Tobey turned to me and said, "It was good to see Zoe again. There will never be anyone like her in this world!"

WHEN ZOE DIED in 1972, I talked with LaMar Harrington, director of the Henry Art Gallery, about establishing a memorial collection in Zoe's name. It would include works by those artists Zoe had known as personal friends, many of whom she had represented as a dealer—works by Stanley William Hayter, Karl Otto Gotz, Bernard Schultze, Sonia Delaunay, Robert West, Claire Falkenstein, Mark Tobey, Pehr Hallsten, Helmi Juvonen, Guy Anderson, John Franklin Koenig, and others. Artist Guy Anderson and his dealer Francine Seders donated one of Guy's most beautiful paintings to the Dusanne Memorial Collection. Henry Art Gallery director LaMar Harrington exhibited these works in a memorial show in the two small rooms at the front of the museum.

Dominating one of the exhibition rooms was a large, not quite life-size photograph of Zoe standing in her Lakeview Boulevard gallery. I sat alone in the Henry Art Gallery exhibition room, looking at this photograph, remembering Zoe. Two elderly ladies came into the room and began to scrutinize the works. When they saw the photograph of Zoe, they looked her over carefully from head to toe. "She certainly had fine ankles!" one of them exclaimed. Zoe would have appreciated such an observation. The ladies continued to look at the works and read the labels. "Look at how many works Mr. Wehr has given this museum. He must be very rich if he can afford to give so many pictures away!" exclaimed one of the women.

I was unshaven, wearing an army jacket. I looked like a bum. Hearing "Mr. Wehr" described as being rich was a bit much. I let out a muffled, derisive snort.

The ladies spun around, staring at me indignantly. "You should show more respect for Mr. Wehr," one of them snapped.

"Believe me, ladies, I know Mr. Wehr very well. Please take my word for it. He just doesn't deserve all that much respect," I explained to them.

LaMar Harrington, the director, appeared in the doorway. "Oh, there you are, Wes. I heard you were here," she said.

The two ladies were dumbfounded. "Are you Mr. Wehr? You can't be! You're dressed like some vagrant!" one of them exclaimed.

"I know," I answered. "But let me put it this way. I've had to choose between spending my money on new clothes or spending it on pictures I could give to museums. Aren't you glad I spent my money on the pictures?" The two ladies mulled this over without replying. Looking back at me as if I weren't quite right in the head, they hurried out of the gallery room.

Imogen Cunningham
in San Francisco

IMOGEN CUNNINGHAM is usually identified with San Francisco, and rightly so. She moved there from Seattle in 1917, at the age of thirty-four, and died there in 1976, at the age of ninety-three. Her life and career began, however, in the Pacific Northwest. She was born in Portland, Oregon, in 1883 and moved with her family to Seattle ten years later. After graduating from the University of Washington in 1907 with honors in chemistry, she lived on Queen Anne Hill. For two years she worked in Edward S. Curtis's photography studio in Seattle and then opened her own successful portrait studio in the same city.

Eve Repentant, her 1910 photograph of a naked Eve, was published in the Seattle magazine, *Town Crier*. It caused an unprecedented sensation. Her 1915 photographs of her husband, etcher Roi Partridge — nude studies taken on Mount

Rainier—were a landmark for their time. Valuable and coveted collectors' items now, they were not especially appreciated during the early years of this century.

Unlike many other "living legends" and "monuments," Miss Cunningham was not one to rest on the fading laurels of a long and distinguished past. From the beginning to the very end of her career, she was always a pioneer in the art and innovations of photography. Her portraits of artist Morris Graves and poet Theodore Roethke, done in 1950 and the early 1970s, are memorable. She maintained close ties with the Pacific Northwest through her good friendships with such people as art scholar and historian Elizabeth Bailey Willis, photographer Mary Randlett, silversmith Ruth Penington, and publisher Don Ellegood, now director emeritus of the University of Washington Press.

She and I had several friends in common. Although I was in and out of San Francisco frequently, the opportunity to meet her never seemed to arise. Finally, in 1972, I decided to telephone her, introduce myself, and attempt to meet her. There was something of a risk in doing this. I had been warned she could be either charming and cordial, or witheringly cool and acerbic. During our phone conversation she invited me, to my surprise, to visit her. This was perhaps because I had mentioned to her that I had studied verse-writing with Theodore Roethke and had known Morris Graves for many years.

Miss Cunningham's small house, set back from the street and surrounded by a large garden, was halfway up Green Street, one of those steep inclines at the western edge of Nob Hill. After separating from Roi Partridge, she had moved to San Francisco in 1943. Before that, she had lived for twenty years near Mills College in Oakland, where her husband was chairman of the art department.

I liked Miss Cunningham's home immediately. The small sitting-room was filled with books and flowers from her own garden. It was not an overdone showplace. It was a real home, casual and comfortable. She offered me a chair and then sat on a sofa facing me. She had a pencil and a small notebook in her lap. During our previous phone conversation, she had jotted down some notes. She quickly glanced at those notes.

"I hope you don't mind. My memory isn't as good as I would want it to be," she said, "so I sometimes take a few notes when I'm talking with a visitor. It saves me a lot of bother later when I'm trying to remember exactly what they said. You told me on the phone that you're a painter. I've known quite a few painters. But, tell me, how do you make a living?"

"But, Miss Cunningham, I told you I'm a painter!" I answered.

There was something in Miss Cunningham's eyes that made it clear she had no sympathy for whiners. Alerted by this, my answer was something of a bluff.

"You make a living from being a painter?"

"Yes, of course. Not always a very good one. But most of the time at least enough to keep me going. One way or another."

Miss Cunningham stared intently at me, a bit suspicious. She broke into laughter.

"Well, I've always made a living as a photographer. Sometimes my family will volunteer to help me out a bit. But I don't need it. I'm quite capable of supporting myself. Young man, it sounds to me as if you and I just may have something in common: we're both practical!"

Imogen Cunningham, 1966 (Photograph by Lynn Harrison,
UW18499, courtesy of University of Washington Libraries)

She put her pencil and notepad on the table next to her, saying: "If you'll excuse me for a moment, I have some fruit juice and cookies in the kitchen. I'll get them, and then we can continue talking."

Miss Cunningham returned a few moments later with a small tray of refreshments. I was dying for a cup of coffee, and I certainly didn't dare ask if I might smoke a cigarette. She served me a small glass of orange juice and a few ginger-snaps. I made a special effort not to wolf them down.

"Now, where were we? Oh, yes. Have you seen Morris Graves lately?" she continued.

"Not for several years. He comes to Seattle now and then, but only when he has to. I write to him, but he's not very good about answering my letters."

"I would assume the demands on his time keep him quite busy. I do know about that sort of thing. I used to phone various friends, but, one way or another, they'd be too busy to see me. Now that I'm something of a local celebrity, those same people will phone asking if I can spare some time to see *them*? I don't mean to sound sour. That's just the way some people are."

I WAS SURPRISED at how quickly I felt at ease with this "living legend." She had brushed aside the usual amenities and talked about what interested her the most. Compared with her brightness, I felt rather pastel. I asked her if she had done any new portrait studies?

"I won't photograph anyone who doesn't like himself. If I do, no matter how I photograph them, they're not going to like the results. They'll complain that the angle isn't quite right, or that I should have tried a different kind of lighting.

What they really mean is that the photograph isn't flattering enough to suit them. With people who *like* themselves, it's a different matter. I can concentrate on the photograph. I don't have to contend with overly complicated egos. So many people want me to photograph them now. Some of them are very rich and will offer me quite a large fee to do it. But I have a fairly good income from my work. I don't have to photograph people who don't interest me. I just don't have time for that sort of thing!"

MY SMALL GLASS of orange juice was empty. I had eaten the gingersnaps as slowly as I could. Miss Cunningham took note of this and brought me more refreshments from the kitchen. The conversation continued.

"Miss Cunningham, is there a chance I might buy one of your photographs while I'm here today?" My inquiry surprised and clearly pleased her.

"I don't see why not. I could arrange for you to do that. Is there some particular one you'd like to buy?"

"I'd especially like to have one of your photographs of Theodore Roethke."

"That's an easy enough matter. My contact prints of Theodore are on the shelf next to where you're sitting," she said.

Miss Cunningham went quickly through an album and handed me contact-sheets of photographs she had taken of Roethke. I didn't want to take up too much of her time or appear overly indecisive. I made the quickest and most obvious choice: her best-known portrait of Roethke.

"How much is the photograph?" I asked.

"I'm afraid it will have to be $100 for the print. I'm sorry it's so expensive, but my gallery sets the prices. Ansel

[Adams] gets $200 for his photographs!" she explained, almost apologetically.

"Do you make your own prints?" I asked.

"Yes, I think that's important. There are other photographers who seem to think their work is finished as soon as they've clicked the shutter. Their prints look like it. Judging from some of the prints they let out, they don't know anything about the quality of a print. They all look alike: impersonal and manufactured. I just can't respect that kind of photographer."

I had recently seen a book of Thomas Eakins's photographs and liked them very much.

"What about Thomas Eakins's photographs? Don't they have a personal quality?" I asked.

"I can see why you might like them; you're a painter. But I don't especially like them myself. I'll grant they're poetic, but they're not my idea of a real photograph," she said.

A week or so before I met Miss Cunningham, I had met a young photographer in Seattle. His photographs seemed humdrum to me.

"Not long ago I met a young photographer. He told me he wants his photographs to be as impersonal as possible. He wants, he told me, only the truth and reality of his subject," I told her.

"I've heard that sort of talk before, and it's just a lot of nonsense. The photographer will always be part of the photograph," she responded, sounding irritated.

Miss Cunningham reflected for a moment and then continued: "Many, many years ago a friend of mine photographed a hawk in the sky. It was fierce and alive!" She raised her arms winglike in the air and looked intently at me with a wild, predatory stare. Her frailty vanished. For an instant she became that hawk. The transformation was electrifying. She then lowered her arms and took a sip of orange juice. She spoke softly, but her eyes had narrowed: "Just a week or so ago, I went to see an exhibition of photographs here in San Francisco. One of the photographs was of a hawk. But the photographer had turned her hawk into a lit-tle ti-ny dick-ie bird! No one can tell me that photographers don't leave a trace of themselves in everything they photograph. I hope your friend in Seattle snaps out of it pretty soon. He's just deluding himself!"

QUITE A BIT OF IMOGEN Cunningham's work survives from the Seattle days. Although she destroyed most of the old glass plates before she moved to San Francisco in 1917, her negatives survive. They are on file with The Imogen Cunningham Trust, administered by her three sons, Gryffyd, Rondal, and Padraic Partridge. I asked Miss Cunningham about her years in Seattle, "I know that you worked with Edward Curtis while you lived in Seattle. And you have an assistant now. But how does one go about teaching photography?"

"There's so much that one can learn only by years of trial and error — by experience, practical experience. Having lots of fancy theories is no substitute for it. A friend of mine who teaches photography sent me some essays his students had written about photography. When I got through reading them, I wrote him back and asked: 'Are you teaching philosophy or photography?'"

SEVERAL DAYS LATER I returned to Miss Cunningham's house. The print of the Roethke portrait was ready. I could pick it up that afternoon. I told her that I would probably donate it later to the University of Washington's photography collection. We talked for a while, but I didn't want to overstay my welcome. As I started to get up from my chair to leave, Miss Cunningham looked at me with sudden intensity, with a look of unguarded near-despair. "I don't like being old, Mr. Wehr. I don't like it at all," she said. There was great dignity and openness in her voice as she continued: "It means I have to be so very careful to conserve my energy now. There are so many things I want to do, and only so much that I now can do. Mr. Wehr, I have enjoyed our visits. When you get back to Seattle, please do write if you have the time. I can't guarantee that I'll answer, or if I do, it may likely be just a short note."

When I bought the Roethke photograph from Miss Cunningham she had been unexpectedly thoughtful, telling me, "Mr. Wehr, I know what it's like when one is traveling, how expensive travel can be. You can send me the money for the photograph when you get back to Seattle. That will be perfectly fine with me and perhaps a little easier on your travel budget."

I had brought with me that afternoon a copy of a book containing many of her most famous photographs. It included portraits of Morris Graves and Theodore Roethke. When I asked Miss Cunningham to autograph this book for me, she inscribed it: "For Wesley Wehr, a friend of some of my favorites." She was referring to Morris Graves and Theodore Roethke. Among all the people I have known, either for many years or even briefly, I would describe Imogen Cunningham as one of my own favorites.

SOME POETS &
A PHILOSOPHER

Theodore Roethke
in the Classroom

I STUDIED WITH POET Theodore Roethke from October 1950 until the spring of 1953. Several of my fellow music students had somehow found their way into his poetry workshop. They came back to the Music Department to spread the word: there was a great teacher, a poet, in the English Department who welcomed musicians, especially composers, into his classes. Musicians, said Roethke, would readily understand what he meant about the musical nature of poetry.

My ears pricked up. I had composed mostly chamber music and piano works, but my real interest lay in composing vocal music. I had no interest in writing poetry, let alone in being a poet. But I wanted to know more about the relationship of words to music. When I read Roethke's poems, I sensed how well they would lend themselves to musical settings. The poetry I later set to music in my graduate thesis, *Nine Songs for Voice and Orchestra*, included poems by Roethke, Edith Sitwell, Kenneth Patchen, and the nineteenth-century poet Ernest Dowson.

I was intrigued by the idea of studying music, even if indirectly, with such an accomplished and well-known poet. Intending to take only a few courses from him, I signed up for Roethke's poetry workshop and survey classes in fall quarter, 1950. He was so effective as a teacher that I ended up re-enrolling in his courses for three years.

Roethke's national reputation as a highly original poet and a first-rate teacher attracted students from far and wide. James Wright, Albert Herzing, and Lloyd Parks came from Ohio to study with him, after studying at Kenyon College with poet John Crowe Ransom. Richard Selig traveled to Seattle from Washington, D.C. Before joining the U.W. English Department faculty, poet David Wagoner had studied with Roethke at Pennsylvania State University.

The Winter 1951 issue of *Poetry Chicago* featured two poetry workshops: the workshop conducted by Paul Engel at the University of Iowa, and Roethke's workshop in Seattle. For this issue, Roethke and Engel each wrote an introductory essay describing their roles as poetry teachers. The remainder of the issue was devoted to poems written by their students.

During the October 1950 class, fellow student Richard Selig sat at one end of the classroom's long table, and I sat next to him. At the opposite end of the table sat Roethke. There was room for only about fourteen students around this table, so the remaining students sat in chairs that lined the two long walls of the classroom. The classroom windows

*Theodore Roethke in his verse writing workshop, University of
Washington, 1962 (Photograph by Duncombe, UW18500,
courtesy of University of Washington Libraries)*

looked out past a small greenhouse onto a view of the campus madrona trees and the Henry Art Gallery. In the following years, other poets would teach in this same room, at this same table—Elizabeth Bishop, Richard Eberhart, Rolfe Humphries, Louise Bogan, Léonie Adams, Vernon Watkins, and Galway Kinnell.

DURING THE FIRST WEEK of class, a student put up his hand.

"Yes, Elmer. What is it?" Roethke asked him.

"Mr. Roethke, what do we have to do to get an A in this class?"

"An A! You are talking about the sacred grade! I just don't hand out that sort of grade easily," he exclaimed, adding, "but since you've asked, I'll tell you what you will have to do to get an A out of Papa Roethke. For openers, I want five poems, all of which are good enough to be published in the best poetry journals in this country. Second, you and your poems are going to have to take me places I've never been before. And, believe me, I've been around. Elmer, if you can deliver like that, I just may give you an A!"

Undaunted, another student put up his hand. "How do we go about writing poems?" he asked.

Roethke raised a finger to the ceiling. "Ah! You want to know how to write a poem. Well, there are lots of ways of going about writing poems. I don't care how you get your poem. That's your business. As far as I'm concerned, you can stick a piece of chalk in your navel and dance up and down in front of the barn door. If you end up writing a poem on the barn door, good. All I want is that you kids go out and get that poem! And I will add, if you're going to be in this class, get ready to give like you've never given before — or get out!" Richard Selig and I looked at each other and fastened our mental safety belts. We were in for a turbulent ride. When the class met again two days later, several students had already fled.

A few weeks later, one of the students read an extraordinarily dull poem to our class. When he had finished, Roethke exclaimed, "My God, that's a boring poem! What did you think you were doing, anyway?"

"But, Mr. Roethke, my poem is *about* boredom!" the student protested.

Roethke was nonplussed. "Don't you realize that it takes enormous poetic energy to convey the quality of boredom?"

Another memorably bad poem was about suffering. Roethke groaned as the student read his poem to the class. Exasperated, he announced, "There will be no more routine suffering in this class. If you've got to suffer, you'd better make your suffering interesting to the rest of us, or leave it at home. We all suffer. If you're going to bring your suffering into my class, make it interesting!"

One of our next assignments was to read some "bad" poetry. By that, Roethke meant sentimental doggerel.

"Why should we read bad poetry when we're trying to learn how to write good poetry?" asked one of his students.

"When you read a lousy poem by anybody else, you may realize that it's the poem you were just about to write. It can save you a lot of wasted time," Roethke explained. He added a bit of advice I especially liked: "Now don't go and fall in love with your poem just because it's your own baby. If it were somebody else's baby you'd say to yourself, 'What an ugly, dumb-looking kid that one is!'"

Roethke's students often began the quarter by writing rather timid and bland poems. But within several weeks some of them made great strides. They began to surprise Roethke and even themselves. Though Roethke was always technically exacting, he was supportive and encouraging with his fledgling students. In fact, he could become fervently excited by something one of his students had written. When a poem pleased or delighted him, his enthusiasm knew no bounds, and his students responded to this combination of technical discipline and personal encouragement.

I DISCOVERED some extraordinary things about Roethke's teaching. The technical training he gave us often paralleled what I was being taught by composers George McKay and John Verrall. I was composing a piano sonata at the time. It contained a passage in the key of A major, a bright and outgoing kind of musical "color." I made an abrupt transition to an entirely different musical key, C sharp minor, a bittersweet tonality. The adagio movement that followed was to be in this same key. Verrall alerted me not to introduce a musical key prematurely. "You brought in a little bit of this musical color too soon. When you get to your adagio, you will have already anticipated and spoiled the freshness and surprise of this C sharp minor key. You threw away your musical effect," he said.

Studying with Roethke, I learned that, even as musical modulations had to be planned very carefully, so shifts of diction in a poem had to be controlled. I had written a stanza with many broad, sustained sounds — many m's and n's. The stanza had a certain tone to it. Then, in the same stanza, I introduced an abrupt shift of tone and diction — harsher sounds, dentates such as "dog," "dental," "delight," or "decimate." "No, no, no! You ruined the effect here," said Roethke. "*Listen* to your poem! You must control these shifts of texture!"

Similarly, when I played a musical passage too harshly, my piano teacher Lockrem Johnson would admonish me: "This whole section is supposed to be played very legato, very smooth and unruffled. But you overaccented those chords. You broke the musical surface. Those accents have to be softened."

Or Mark Tobey, my painting teacher, would tell me that one of his problems in painting was knowing "how to accent without the accent detaching itself from the picture plane." I felt as if a window were opening. These technical problems of accentuation in poetry, music, and painting had elements in common. I was gaining an exciting new perspective.

Roethke might also point out that a certain word in a student's poem was not "musically right." "I know this word *means* just about what you want it to convey. But that's not enough. The words you select should have an auditory rightness. Their tonal properties—the *sound* of each word—should contribute to the meaning and effect of what you're trying to say." He stressed the importance of the sonorities of language. He referred often to critic Kenneth Burke's work while he taught us about the qualities of words—about their weight, their sound, the speed with which they were spoken. This was one of the most technically demanding and precise aspects of his teaching, this attention to the comparative *weight* of a word. Is it a "heavy-sounding" word, or is it a word quickly and lightly spoken? And he constantly asked us: "Does the movement and tempo of your poem enhance what you're talking about, what you're trying to *express*?"

This approach to writing poetry placed new demands on any young poet who might have thought that "expressing oneself" implied a degree of self-indulgence. Roethke was insisting that we build our poems as carefully as a composer constructed a musical composition. Our apprenticeship was a highly controlled process. When we first started writing in his class, Roethke immediately put us to work writing some very elementary couplets, quatrains, and short stanzas. My first poetic exercise for him consisted of a simple lyric: "Sound by sound / root out the bound / echo of an old song / unmuted even yet." It really creaked along, I guess. But that was how we began.

ROETHKE'S OWN FIRST BOOK, *Open House* (1941), contained many highly formal poems, lapidary models of conciseness. He was learning his craft from the ground floor up, honing himself as he wrote these poems — much as Elizabeth Bishop would instruct her own students for their first assignment in 1966: "I want something very tidy and neat — like a hymn."

If a line of poetry had what psychologist Jerome Bruner called "effective surprise," Roethke would say, "This line has the proper nuttiness." He never formulated for us what he meant by that, but we more-or-less knew what he was getting at. Something mysterious, but evocative. Strange, but somehow right. In that respect, his teaching worked a kind of osmosis. "Listen, listen very *carefully* to this poem!" he kept telling us, as he gradually taught us how to pay much more attention to what we were doing. He took us into great poetry and permeated us with it. He read great poems aloud to us in class. He urged us to read as much poetry as possible.

ROETHKE HAD OF COURSE GIVEN a great deal of thought and planning to how he structured his classes. After the initial, very simple verse-writing assignments, when he felt we were on more solid ground technically, he took us step-by-step into writing poetry in more difficult forms — a sonnet, a villanelle, a sestina. The assignments and challenges were carefully paced, each leading to the next one. Before we tackled writing in any of these technically complex modes, he read us examples of what other poets had done with these forms. After giving us a particularly difficult assignment he would sometimes say, "I think teacher had better see if he's any good at this." He tested anew his own control of these forms by trying his hand at the same assignments he gave his students.

Roethke's exams could be alarmingly difficult. Sometimes I felt we were in some kind of poetry boot camp, being subjected to the toughest exercises imaginable. The various lines of poetry to identify could be relatively easy. But then there might be two opening lines of a poem. We were to finish the poem in the style of those two opening lines. There might be a page with scattered words on it. We were to write a coherent poem around those words, incorporating them into the poem in such a way that they seemed to belong there naturally. We were to write poems with no adjectives in them. When I had finally taken all the exams Roethke had previously prepared, he told me, "Just go home, Wehr. Forget about taking another exam. You've already taken every exam I have in my files. I'm not going to make up a new exam just for you."

ROETHKE WAS EMPHATIC when he explained to us that only rarely if ever during a poet's lifetime does a good poem appear intact and effortlessly. This was reinforced for me in 1953, when Oscar Williams, the poetry anthologist, visited the university. Mr. Williams handed me a bulky envelope to hold while he was talking to our class. Was it the manuscript for a long Russian novel? No, it was the original worksheets for a single poem, Dylan Thomas's "In the White Giant's Thigh." All those pages and pages for a sixty-line poem!

Many noted poets came to visit Roethke in Seattle, some of whom he invited to attend his class. One afternoon, he arrived, announcing, "Kids, I have a great surprise for you. You are about to meet William Carlos Williams, himself!" Dr. Williams came into the room and began conversing with Roethke, but we students were too awed by the mere presence of him to ask any questions. Only Richard Selig had the wherewithal and composure to initiate with him a brief discussion about poetry.

ROETHKE'S GARGANTUAN public struggles with cycles of elation and depression are well known and legendary. For better or for worse, the anecdotes are many and colorful. It becomes all the more important, therefore, to emphasize his highly organized, articulate, and sensitive presence in our classroom. His brilliant effectiveness as a teacher was of the highest order. I loathed all the slanted stuff that was building up the Roethke myth. Those great poems of his didn't come out of disorder and bedlam. They were written during times of extreme focus and lucidity. Roethke's tortured-poet image obscured this other important side of his nature. When an artist is really at his greatest he is often a rather colorless sort, working painstakingly hard at trying to make the poem better, and still better. But that everyday hard work doesn't make for a very exciting biography. The day-to-day toiling and trudging are often left out, overlooked, ignored.

There was much about creativity itself and the hard work of it that one could learn from Roethke: different approaches to knowing oneself — one's own ego, one's vanity, vulnerability, and pride — and how to collaborate with them. He was alert to all those aspects of the psyche that might either inspire great poetry or drive a poet into a bad corner. We learned ways in which a poet could release creative energy, or could sidestep a creative block. This was one of the lasting effects of working with him. So many writers and artists passively accept the so-called creative block as some kind of punishment from their muse or private demons. As philosopher Susanne K. Langer once remarked to me: "Most people are entirely oblivious to the distinction between bad results and punishment."

And we learned from some of his students. A middle-aged African American woman took part in our 1951 poetry workshop. She had raised a family, found that she loved poetry, and decided to take a poetry class. I don't recall her name. She said very little in class. She sat in the background, listening carefully to everything said by Roethke and the students. Weeks went by. Finally one afternoon she raised her hand, "Mr. Roethke, I have a poem now. May I read it to the class?"

"Of course, my dear. Please do. We would be honored," he answered.

"All right," she said. "Here is my poem." It consisted, in its entirety, of twelve plainspoken words: "Love is a river. At the end of it sits a beggar."

We sat silent. We had all been trying so hard to craft poems that would impress the class and win approval from

Roethke. This poem humbled us. It was disarmingly direct, brief, and genuine.

Roethke beamed, and looked at the woman with gentle admiration. "That, my dear," he said with obvious affection, "is a true poem. You honor us by your presence in this classroom."

ROETHKE OFTEN READ poetry aloud to us, poems by Gerard Manley Hopkins, John Donne, the Elizabethans, Federico García Lorca, Wallace Stevens, Louise Bogan, Léonie Adams, William Butler Yeats, Hart Crane, and many other poets. When he came to a passage he especially liked, he'd stop and read it again to us, slowly and deliberately. "Listen very *carefully* to this!" he'd say. It could be a line from Wallace Stevens: "How quick she comes in slipper green." "Listen to that effect! That line *sounds* like the movement of a quick footstep!" It was very much like studying with a most exacting musician.

One afternoon Roethke read to us Hopkins's "The Leaden Echo and the Golden Echo." It was one of the great poetic experiences to hear him read that poem aloud. When he came to the final lines, nearly whispering, "Yonder.— What high as that! We follow now, we follow , , ," we felt we had glimpsed eternity itself.

Another time he read one of John Donne's *Holy Sonnets*. A lot of major excavation and construction was going on next to our Parrington Hall classroom. The workmen were building utility tunnels. Meanwhile, Roethke was thundering his way through the Donne sonnet. It was a tumultuous performance. Just as he got to the final line, an explosive charge went off, shaking Parrington Hall as if to its very foundations.

He looked reverently up past the classroom ceiling to an imaginary celestial sky above us. "Thank you, dear Lord. I'm so glad you approve of the way I read that!"

Roethke paced back and forth as he read, waving his hands in the air like an orchestra conductor. He was a very large man. But he took an apparent delight in becoming rather elfin, too. I think he relished the contrast between his physical formidability and the tenderness and delicacy with which he could read a lyric poem. Try to imagine an elephant conducting Mozart superbly.

Did Roethke read his own poetry to his class, or use it in his teaching? He might read or send a new poem to a close friend, usually a fellow poet, but I don't recall his reading his own work to his class while he was teaching. On one occasion, however, he did ask fellow student James Wright and me to stay after class. He had just written part of his Sir John Davies series of four poems, and he wanted to try the new material out on Jim and me.

Roethke had a long apprenticeship with poets Louise Bogan and Rolfe Humphries, and with critic Kenneth Burke. He routinely sent them his own poems for criticism. It wasn't until many years later, when I read the collected letters of both Roethke and Louise Bogan, that I realized he had long ago been Bogan's lover. While I was studying with him, I sent a group of my poems to Miss Bogan for comment. I didn't know much about her except that Roethke had read us many of her poems, and I thought they were superb. Several weeks later a handwritten letter from Miss Bogan arrived in my mailbox. "Dear Mr. Wehr," she wrote, "I have a policy of never commenting upon poems which are sent to me in the mail. However, I can say that if you are studying with

Theodore Roethke, you are in the best of hands. Sincerely, Louise Bogan."

I showed this letter to Roethke. He read it, grinned broadly, exclaiming: "Ahh, the old dear. She ain't forgotten!"

KEEPING STUDENT NOTEBOOKS was mandatory, an important part of our classwork. And, as Roethke reminded us, an important part of our grade. We saved all of our revisions, and included poems we liked, anything about poetry that we wanted to remember, a favorite quote from somebody. When he went through our notebooks, he could tell a lot about our progress or lack of it. These notebooks are now with the Theodore Roethke papers at the University of Washington Library's Manuscripts and University Archives Division. Several years ago I asked to see Richard Selig's student poems and my own. On the margins of the pages, Roethke had written such comments as "maudlin!" "cliché!" or "good line!" All of these marginal notes, by the way, are now literary estate property.

Now and then one of his students would come up with a line or an image that Roethke really liked. "I'll buy that line from you," he'd say, fishing into his pocket for some small change. The idea that Roethke would offer to buy a scrap of poetry from us seemed both flattering and practical— especially when we watched the financial transaction taking place right in the class.

DID ANY OF Roethke's students imitate him? Richard Selig certainly didn't. Nor did James Wright. Nor, for that matter, did Carolyn Kizer, Robert Sund, Lloyd Parks, or Albert Herzing. No, I don't remember anyone imitating Roethke's poetry. On the other hand, I don't think he would have necessarily discouraged this. There is, after all, a lot to be learned from imitating other poets. But it is to his credit as a teacher that his students were not rubber stamps.

How encouraging and supportive of his students was Roethke? At first he was surprisingly generous with his praise for what I wrote. But then my poems became so stilted and self-conscious that even I could see that something was very wrong with them. I ran into him on the front steps of Parrington Hall. I had just written a first draft of another poem, and I wanted to show it to him. His face sank as he read it. He got out his fountain pen and scratched out one line after another. He crossed out nearly half a page. "This is where your poem really starts. All this other stuff is just a warm-up," he told me. He had also circled a line that caught his attention: "We sing our praises to the mineral kingdom." And that line, he told me, was barely under the wire. He looked at me sadly, visibly pained. "Wehr, I could show you how to improve this poem. I could show you how to fix it up. But I'm not going to. It's not a good poem. You've written some good poems. I just don't know why your new work is so disappointing. Even though I could make this poem better, you wouldn't understand why and how I had improved it. It isn't the poem that needs changing. It's you who is going to have to change first, and then the poem will follow." Though Roethke had often helped us with our revisions, he told me that the problems with the poems I was writing went beyond mere craft. I was bewildered. How was I to go about "changing" myself? In what way? I wrote very little poetry after that. I went back to composing music.

Richard
Selig

— FROM THE 16TH FLOOR —

Pardoning this borough for its evil,
I look past the tops of buildings, to where
The sky is. Remembering that man's malice,
This man's fate; the former's cunning,
The latter's jeopardy — seeing the sky,
Placid in spite of soot and heartache,
I am reminded to pray. Redemption,
Like our janitor, comes as we go home:
A stooped man turning out the lights.

— RICHARD SELIG

New York City, 1957

T HE FIRST DAY of Theodore Roethke's autumn 1950 verse writing class, Richard Selig walked into the classroom, took a seat next to mine, shuffled through his sheaf of poems, and introduced himself to me: "My name is Richard Selig. I've come here from Washington, D.C., to study with Theodore Roethke. Who are you?"

He had already forgotten that two days earlier he had waited on me and several of my friends at a small restaurant down the street. Wearing a food-stained waiter's uniform, he appeared at our table to take our orders. We were, to his mind, taking too long to decide on what we wanted. He made no bones about telling us so. Even though his voice was gruff and impatient, its resonance was startling. Richard, however, was not cut out to be a waiter. A few days later he found a more interesting job working in John Uitti's frame shop on University Way.

Richard Selig was born in New York City on October 29, 1929—on Black Tuesday, the day of the stock market crash. The celebrated Irish singer Mary O'Hara, his widow, has written in her autobiography a detailed account of his life (*The Scent of the Roses*, London: Joseph Malone, 1980). He grew up on Long Island. In his teens his family moved to Washington, D.C. After high school, he started wandering. He studied psychology at Occidental College in Los Angeles, followed by a year on a painting scholarship with the Museum of Modern Art in New York City. He spent a year studying French at the Sorbonne. During 1950–53, he completed a degree in English at the University of Washington and taught there for a year on a teaching fellowship. Richard had, in fact, traveled around so much by the time I met him in 1950 that his three years in Seattle seemed like an unusually long stay.

Richard arrived in Seattle by bus from Washington, D.C., only one week before the start of Roethke's fall quarter classes. The poetry workshop met three days a week. Richard plunged into writing new poetry. Like those of Roethke, W. B. Yeats, or Dylan Thomas, his poems were lyric, bardic, and oracular. They were well-tailored to his distinctively individual voice.

When I first met Richard, I lived in a single room in the Kennedy Building next to the University District post office. My furnishings consisted of a small bed, a writing desk and chair, and an upright piano. Richard lived in an even smaller room at the College Inn, three blocks down University Way. He had just enough space for a bed, a table, and a chair. For cooking, he used a hot plate, a frying pan, and a cast-iron kettle into which he continually added vegetables and bits of meat for an ongoing Irish stew.

In the fabled kingdom of my heart
The Hawk pursues his love,
Breaks from the sky with talons hooked
To claim the tender dove.

No hawk knows better grace
Nor dove a deeper pain
Than I, alone in this dark place,
Loved by beasts of the brain.
—from THREE SONGS
January 1951

Richard Selig, before he left Seattle for England, 1953
(Photograph courtesy of Mary O'Hara Selig)

When Richard wrote a new poem, he was usually impatient to try it out on me. His soft, insistent knock on my door late at night often woke me from a deep sleep, "Wes, it's Richard. Wake up. I have a new poem to show you. It can't wait until morning."

Bleary-eyed, I unlocked the door. Richard entered quickly and sat on the edge of my bed, reading his poem to me. Had I written any new poems? If so, where were they?

If I had just written a new poem, no matter how late at night it happened to be, I similarly headed down University Way to show it to him. One night, around midnight, I knocked on his door.

"Who's there?" he asked, sounding irritated.

"It's me—Wes."

"Do you have a new poem with you?"

"Yes, two new poems."

"All right, I'll be right there."

He answered the door in his boxer shorts. There was someone in his bed. Richard, it appeared, was busy entertaining a young lady. So that I wouldn't chance to recognize her from several parties he and I attended together, Richard had quickly thrown a blanket over her "This is important. I'll get back to you as soon as I can. Take a nap!" he instructed her. He carefully read through my manuscript, pointing out where and how he thought I could improve it. We must have spent at least forty minutes going over my five-stanza poem. At times like that I realized how dedicated a poet Richard was. His lady friend could wait. Poetry could not!

RICHARD WAS AN extraordinarily articulate and quick student. Besides taking Roethke's poetry courses, he took classes

from historian Giovanni Costigan and studied French sym-
bolist poetry with Jackson Matthews. He impressed both
Costigan and Matthews as being a brilliant student. He was
also, if necessary, a brilliant bluffer. One morning he came to
Roethke's class looking atypically hungover. He must have
forgotten he was supposed to hold forth on Hart Crane's poem
"Santa Maria" that particular day. Richard's hastily improvised interpretation of the poem was ponderous and scholarly.
Roethke sat with a bemused look while Richard droned on. It
was clear to him that Richard had likely not even looked at
the poem until that moment.

When Richard finished his off-the-cuff discourse on the
many symbolic levels of Hart Crane's poem, Roethke said:
"Well, Richard, you may not know much about this poem,
but I do have to give you high marks for one of the best jobs
of bluffing I've seen to date in this class. Believe me, that's saying a lot!" Not being prepared that morning in class had been
an exception for Richard. Most of the time he burned the
midnight oil. If he had not been a first-rate student, his teachers would not have recommended him so highly for a Rhodes
scholarship the following year.

I INTRODUCED RICHARD to painter Mark Tobey. Once
a month, Tobey invited his friends to an evening open house,
and he had suggested I invite Richard to come along. They
soon became good friends. Richard would later characterize
that friendship in a letter from England (1955) to his bride-to-
be, Irish singer Mary O'Hara: "Sir John [Gielgud] is one of
that rare, amazing ilk, the pure artist. I've known only two
others to equal him, Mark Tobey, the painter, and Roethke.
The surge of their thoughts is an experience I have long

missed in this effete, self-conscious, and too-sophisticated community."

DURING THE SPRING quarter of 1953, American poet Richard Eberhart came to teach at the University of Washington. One week Eberhart's friend, anthologist Oscar Williams, visited our class. Williams's anthologies of modern poetry were popular. Poets vied to be included in them.

Eberhart informed our class that Mr. Williams had consented to meet with each of us privately if we wanted to show him our poems. I had written a creaky villanelle. Mr. Williams went over it with me. He was cordial and encouraging. Despite his being a highly influential anthologist, I found him to be somewhat self-effacing, perhaps even shy. As Mr. Williams went through my poem, I glanced into the hallway. Richard sat alone near the window, smoking a cigarette, waiting to show Mr. Williams his poems.

That evening Richard came by my room, offended and infuriated. Mr. Williams had gone over Richard's poems and noticed that many of them bore dedications to Richard's friends. "Williams had the gall," Richard snapped, "to ask me if I were writing poems or Valentines!" Three days later, Mr. Williams revisited our class, bringing with him a copy of the *Daily*, the University of Washington student newspaper. In miffed retaliation for Oscar Williams's slighting remark, Richard had written a limerick. The campus paper had promptly published it. Mr. Williams read the limerick aloud to the class. It began, "There's a wizened old anthologist / Whose anthologies will never be missed." Mr. Williams closed the newspaper. "It's not even a good limerick. It doesn't scan. The rhymes are trite," he said. This story does end well, much to the credit of Oscar Williams. Shortly after Richard died on October 14, 1957, in New York City, Williams anthologized one of Richard's last poems, "From the Sixteenth Floor," in his anthology *A Pocket Book of Modern Verse: English and American Poetry of the Last 100 Years.*

DURING 1951–52, painter Bob West and I shared a small apartment several blocks north of the campus. Richard often visited us. On New Year's Eve 1951, Richard arrived bearing a new poem he had dedicated to Bob and me. I suggested that he record his holiday poem on the old phonographrecorder Bob and I had just acquired. For that matter, said I, why not record a group of his poems. The recording he made that evening, reading thirteen of his poems, became the only surviving document of some of his finest poems.

Shortly before his death in 1957, Richard went through his poems to see if he had enough to warrant publishing a book. He rejected almost all of his earlier poems, including most of those he had written in Seattle. Two of his Seattle poems had, however, been published in the Seattle literary magazine, *Experiment,* in a special issue edited by Richard Eberhart in 1953. Before giving Richard's recording of his Seattle poems to John William Sweeny, curator of the Woodberry Poetry Room Collection at Harvard University in 1967, I transcribed those poems as well.

A small volume of Richard Selig's collected poems, edited by Peter Levi, was published by Dolmen Press in Ireland in 1962. During his lifetime, Richard's poems were published in such English literary journals as *Encounter* and *The Listener,* and in the international journal, *Botteghe Oscure.* The highly influential poet Stephen Spender had, according to Mary O'Hara Selig, "done more than anyone else in England and America to have Richard's work published."

Theodore Roethke wrote a memorial tribute to Richard Selig which was printed in *Encounter*. It was an odd mixture of high praise for Richard's gifts and somewhat negative remarks about Richard's alleged personality traits. Roethke's faculty friends, Arnold Stein and Jackson Matthews, were alarmed when they read the first draft and suggested to him that he tone it down. Roethke was adamant. Richard, he insisted, would have wanted him to tell it as it supposedly was — no sugar coating, death or no death. Roethke at the time, however was hospitalized and undergoing treatment at the Pinel Sanitarium north of Seattle.

The summer of 1953 was a low point during my student years. My roommate Bob West had been given a Fulbright fellowship to study painting at the Slade School in London. He would be gone at least a year. My own application for a Fulbright to study in London was turned down. That same year Richard Selig was awarded a Rhodes scholarship to study at Oxford. Other close friends were also leaving the Northwest. Many of the friends I had grown accustomed to seeing almost daily were scattering to the proverbial winds.

Richard wrote to me from Oxford. He described the setting, the libraries, his fellow students, the restaurants, the kind of room he now lived in. One bit of news was especially exciting: his tutor during his first year at Magdalen College was to be C. S. Lewis, author of *The Screwtape Letters*. Richard and I stayed in touch, exchanging letters now and then. On December 2, 1955, he wrote to his fiancée, Mary O'Hara: "I received a fine letter from my old friend, Wesley Wehr of Seattle: a composer and a young man growing wiser every day. He says: 'Thank God for change and growth—and what a pity that it is to disappoint so many—as if there's time to stand still and be defined by the lazy.'" I had no idea at all when I would ever see Richard again, especially since I rarely strayed far from the Pacific Northwest.

Unexpectedly, my aunt Edna died in Los Angeles in 1953. When my father and I went with my grandmother and the lawyer to open my aunt's safe deposit box, we were astonished to find that Aunt Edna was no pauper. The deposit box held primarily two kinds of documents: ardent love letters— some of them with recent postmarks—and a great quantity of AT&T stock. I was the principal beneficiary. Aunt Edna had attached an informal proviso to my inheriting the telephone stock: I was to sell off part of it and use the money to go to Europe. I wrote Richard immediately that I would head for New York and London as soon as the inheritance came through. It seemed to take forever for the estate to be settled. When I received my money, I caught a plane for New York. By September I was on a boat headed for England.

Richard and Mary O'Hara had meanwhile married and were living in London. They had first met at the Edinburgh Music Festival, where Mary was performing. When I arrived in London, they invited me to stay with them. Later that night, after Mary had retired, Richard said, "Wes, now that Mary has gone to bed, I need to talk to you." He poured me a tumbler full of Irish whiskey. We toasted each other.

"What's up, Richard? You look awfully serious," I asked.

Coming straight to the point, he answered, "The news is not good. I have Hodgkin's disease. It's a cancer of the lymph glands. It's incurable. The doctors give me at most a year or two to live."

I caught my bearings as best I could.

"You are not to tell anyone in Seattle about this," he instructed me, "If anyone there knew how numbered my days are, they'd start being nice to me. That's the *last* thing I want!"

Richard and Mary moved to New York the following year. I returned to New York from Seattle and met Richard for lunch at the Fulton Fish Market. I didn't realize then just how ill he was. While I was visiting philosopher Susanne Langer at Old Lyme soon thereafter, Richard died. When I returned from Connecticut and phoned his apartment, Mary broke the news to me. I stayed in New York just long enough for his funeral and flew home to Seattle the following day.

My first day back on University Way I ran into poet Carolyn Kizer. She had known Richard while he was studying with Roethke in Seattle. I told her what had happened: "Carolyn, I was at Richard Selig's funeral in New York yesterday. He died of Hodgkin's disease. He told me about it when I saw him in London last year."

"Why didn't you tell me Richard was dying? If I had only known, I would have been nicer to him!" she exclaimed.

"But that's exactly what he *didn't* want—people being 'nice' to him!" I explained. Richard had called the cards right on that one.

ONE WINTER EVENING, during the time we were studying with Roethke, Richard sat across from me in a University Way all-night coffee shop. We were having the breakfast special—two hotcakes, one egg, two pieces of bacon, and coffee, all for sixty-nine cents! We were both twenty-one. Turning his palms toward me, Richard raised his hands and contemplated them. "You know, Wes," he said. "We are both young now, and at the beginning of what may be a very long life for both of us. One of us obviously will outlive the other. But neither of us can know now which of us it will be." He grew silent, staring at his hands. He was studying how the lights and shadows played across them as he moved them this way and that. He studied them as a painter would. Noticing how intently I was looking at him, Richard said, "These hands of mine, they seem so present and immediate to me. But contemplating them, I have just realized how mortal and ephemeral you and I actually are." With that, he picked up his fork and continued to eat his breakfast. None of the other customers seemed to notice us. Above us, the restaurant's glaring incandescent lights regarded us impersonally.

Richard was unusual in that one minute he seemed like a perfectly normal young man, enjoying the fullness of being young — writing poetry, partying with his friends, and falling in love. He was different, however. I think Richard, unlike any other young person I had known, had an almost Apollonian detachment and distance from the part of him that was young. I suspected that whenever his time did come, he would probably accept it calmly, as he did six years later. Unlike Richard, I suffered from one of the greatest illusions of being young — a fixed belief that somehow, one way or another, I was personally exempt from mere mortality and had been mysteriously singled out to live forever.

My friendship with Richard was unique for me. None of the stories I have related about him nor my descriptions of him begin to explain why he made such a lasting impression on me. Did he ever, for instance, exhibit sentimentality in any way? No, never. Did I ever feel or suspect that he said anything to me that wasn't an exact expression of his thoughts, opinions, and feelings? Certainly not. His words never seemed to be modified or twisted by some hidden, self-serving purpose. He always said exactly what he thought and felt.

I don't remember now what the occasion was, but I had done something that upset Richard and embarrassed me. When I started to apologize to him, his eyes flashed. "I can readily accept what you did," he told me, "but I can not accept your apology. You were negligent and thoughtless. We are all responsible for our actions. Trying to apologize later is hypocritical. You should not have behaved so badly in the first place. A mere apology is no substitution for consideration." Even when the words stung and weren't at all what I wanted to hear, I could always be glad that he was showing me clearly where I stood with him.

This honesty of his sprang, I believe, from the seriousness with which he regarded friendship. He disliked platitudes. He disliked exaggeration in any form. If his enthusiasm for something I had said or done was expressed in generous praise, I could depend upon his meaning every word of what he said. His compliments, and even his acceptance, meant something because they were not given lightly nor easily granted. What I took at first to be a kind of toughness in him I came to see was a reflection of the high standards Richard exacted from himself and from the people he cared about. Many of the teachers I had during college didn't expect much of me. A few, however, seemed at times unreasonable in what they thought I could do, and eventually become. It's the tough, demanding mentors I remember now. Richard Selig was among the best of them.

Elizabeth Bishop
in Seattle

SHE HAD JUST ARRIVED in Seattle from Brazil. The prospect of teaching a poetry workshop terrified her; she had never done such a thing before. But the University of Washington had made her a very good offer, and her house in Ouro Prêto needed a new roof.

That is how I came to know poet Elizabeth Bishop.

Several days after she appeared in Seattle in early January of 1966, I asked her if I might attend her poetry class. Fortunately, she was amenable. I was curious to know how she would approach poetry in the university classroom. Unlike my former workshop teachers Theodore Roethke and Richard Eberhart, Miss Bishop had not taught the writing of poetry and had no codified way of going about it. To further complicate matters, Theodore Roethke's legendary brilliance as a teacher during his fifteen years (1947–62) on the faculty was a hard act to follow. The sheer power of Roethke's personality, both as a poet and teacher, had permeated the Northwest's literary climate. Miss Bishop was aware that she would be judged by a formidable standard.

It was not easy at first for Miss Bishop to stand her ground. Her students, however, soon accepted how unlike Theodore Roethke she was. He had been dramatic, volatile, overpowering; she was modest, understated, low key. For better or for worse, Roethke had become the role model for many of the young poets in the Northwest, but Elizabeth Bishop was not competing with Roethke or any other contemporary poet to be an oracular presence. She felt strongly that her responsibility as a teacher was to help her students get down to the matter of words and how to use them well.

Her primary concern was that her students realize there was no single formula by which a young writer could become a poet, although there was a common thread. There were distinctive voices and personalities—from the flamboyance of a Dylan Thomas to the quiet presence of a Wallace Stevens or a Marianne Moore. Such differences aside, the good poets all shared in common a gift for powerful poetic insight and a hard-won mastery of their craft.

I FIRST SAW Elizabeth Bishop in Lee's Restaurant on University Way, several days before she began to teach at the university. Her impressive literary reputation—she was Poet Laureate (Consultant in Poetry to the Library of Congress) while she was still in her thirties; she won the Pulitzer Prize in 1955—these and other distinctions had preceded her to Seattle, where one had come to expect dramatic entrances and theatrical flourishes from celebrated poets. She was

A Camano Island picnic at Professor and Mrs. Heilman's beach house, 1966. Front row, left to right, Elizabeth Bishop, poet Rolfe Humphries and Mrs. Humphries, English poet Henry Reed; back row, Robert Heilman and Dorothee Bowie (Photograph by Ruth Heilman, courtesy of University of Washington Libraries)

having lunch with English poet Henry Reed. Another woman, it may have been departmental secretary Dorothee Bowie, was at the table. The three of them were talking quietly and unobtrusively. My first impression of Miss Bishop was odd and immediate — she was not concerned with making an impression. Even at a distance, she struck me as a woman who knew exactly who she was, and who knew as well the exact boundaries of her world.

I went to the University Bookstore the next day to buy a copy of her *Questions of Travel*. I was intrigued by this woman, this distinctive writer. In Roethke's classes some years earlier we had read a few of her poems. I remembered best her poem "Letter to N. Y."—with its taxicab meter that "glares like a moral owl." Who would write, I had wondered, a poem about a taxi ride through Central Park? As Roethke's student, my tastes inclined toward such poets as Yeats, Donne, Hopkins, Crane, Lorca, and Blake — poets who transformed everything they saw into a highly charged personal expression. But now I was reading *Questions of Travel*, and I found myself unprepared for what lay before me in its opening pages. Her poetry was witty, outward looking, sharply visual, without the obsessive self-absorption typical of many other poets. I didn't know that poets wrote poems like Elizabeth Bishop's. Her poems seemed uniquely convincing — and somewhat alien to me.

I BEGAN TO SIT in on her classes and to stay after class now and then to chat with her. I finally invited her out for coffee after class. We walked from Parrington Hall to a restaurant down the street, conversing easily. It turned out we had several mutual acquaintances. We talked about American composer Ned Rorem and his settings of her poetry. She mentioned longevity. "You know," she mused, "I've already outlived the normal life span of my own family." I was surprised by how easy it was to talk with her.

Several days after I first met her, Elizabeth called and asked if I would come over to her motel room on Roosevelt Way. She asked me to pick up a six-pack and bring it along. When I arrived at the motel, Elizabeth answered the door and invited me in. She was in her housecoat. I went into the kitchen and clumsily brought each of us a beer. When I returned to the motel living room, she was sitting in bed. I sat on a chair next to her bed. She looked distraught and unhappy. "I don't know what I'm going to do," she said. "I'm miserable. I don't know if I can go through with this. I'm thinking of canceling the teaching arrangement and going home."

The weather was terrible. January. It was pouring rain, day in, day out. Elizabeth was stuck in a god-awful motel room till she could find an apartment, and she was confronted with a class full of students who were, for the most part, not as widely read in the poetic tradition as she had hoped. She missed her Brazilian friend, Lota. She kept repeating, "My dear Lota, I miss her so much." She was devoted to Lota.

She missed Brazil, although she knew that the money for the roof for the house in Ouro Prêto was important.

"Oh, if you were in Brazil," she sighed, "you would see how beautiful it is where I live!"

She was on the edge of tears as I sat next to the bed, ineptly trying to cheer her up. She noticed my staring at her.

"I look awful. Please don't stare at me. I haven't got my makeup on."

I was bewildered. On such short acquaintance, she was unexpectedly pouring out her anguish to me. "I have a feeling I can trust you," she said, quietly and seriously. I felt that an enormous responsibility came with that word "trust." I've never been able to be precisely sure what the responsibility meant, because I would hear her say at other times, "Please don't be so protective of me!"

I TOOK MANY notes both in class and following my private conversations with Elizabeth. Many of these notes were hastily scrawled on scraps of paper. Later I would transcribe them into my diaries. What follows now are a few accounts of what took place in and out of her classroom during 1966, along with some notes of later times, until her death in 1979.

EACH OF MISS BISHOP'S students was assigned to read a favorite poem to the class. For the most part, what they chose was either a well-known poem by a contemporary poet such as Dylan Thomas or Robert Frost — or some rather sentimental doggerel they had likely come upon in a magazine. The poems were either overly familiar or simply bad.

Finally the self-appointed rebel in the class had his turn. *His* favorite poem was a rambling catalog of four-letter words. He half blurted the poem out, stumbling through it as best he could. It certainly didn't come off as shocking. It merely fell flat. When he finished, he announced militantly: "And *that*, Miss Bishop, is *my* favorite poem!"

Elizabeth Bishop answered calmly, "Well, Mr. Belcher, I don't think that's a good poem."

"You don't like that poem because it's got a lot of obscene words in it you don't like!" the student snapped back at her.

Unruffled, Miss Bishop responded, "Now, Mr. Belcher. That's not *at all* the reason I don't care for that poem. There's nothing intrinsically wrong with those words that you call 'obscene.' After all, whether one personally likes them or not, they *are* a part of the English language! For that matter, there are a few of them in that so-called poem that I myself have sometimes used; that is, when I felt the situation really called for it. But I don't think the writer has used those words well. The poem doesn't shock me. I almost wish it did. It just bored me. That's all."

There was a smattering of applause from the students. Protocol forbade Miss Bishop to acknowledge it. Instead, she continued, "If a poet sets out to be shocking and can't place his words firmly and effectively, he can be sure of one thing, at least: When the initial flurries of dismay have worn thin, what remains is usually tasteless or silly. What you students are in this class for is to learn how to *use* words, not just to toss them about, hitting upon some haphazard effect. So now, let me give you instead something by a writer who *knows* what he's doing." And she read us a few lively excerpts from Geoffrey Chaucer.

MISS BISHOP WAS OFTEN undecided as to how she might best teach the writing of poetry. Shortly after I had started attending her classes, she invited me to join her for dinner at Lee's Restaurant. She wanted to discuss how her classes were going. She thought I might have a few useful suggestions. From the outset, she had realized she would have to direct her students toward observing objects more closely.

"Their poems are too vague. There's a tendency to write a kind of mood poem — about love, loss, dripping leaves, damp moonlight. Sharp, *accurate* observation — that's the essential starting point. I'm going to try a little experiment on my students tomorrow. You're a painter, Wes. You'll understand why I'm doing this," she told me. "I'll bring some ordinary things to class. An old shoe, perhaps, and some kitchen utensils." — I had a sudden, fleeting image of an owl taxicab meter. — "I'll have to give some thought to it," she continued. "I'll ask the students to start writing about those objects right there in class . . focus, write down whatever comes into their heads. I've found that they often write much better under time pressure. I've got to do *something* about shaking them out of their bad habits. . . .

"I'm convinced that the poet's eye is somewhat like that of the painter. And it has to be trained and sharpened to notice the fascinating *differences* between things. Some of my students are writing poems in which I could substitute one object for another, and no one would ever know the difference. Interchangeable adjectives. They tell me nothing *precise*, nothing memorable. . . . You've seen Vermeer's paintings, Wes. The objects in them are precisely observed and rendered. And he is certainly a most arresting and original painter!"

Miss Bishop was also a painter, and a very good one. (A book of all her paintings presently accounted for was published in 1996 — William Benton, *Exchanging Hats: Elizabeth Bishop's Paintings*, New York: Farrar, Straus, Giroux.) Indeed, my friendship with her had really begun with our mutual interest in painting. When I asked to sit in on her poetry classes, I also showed her a few of my own landscape paintings.

"By all means! I would very much like to have a painter in this class!" she had said.

Her plan to have the students write about specific objects was akin to that of an art teacher's having her students sketch from the model and from nature. It was an exercise in observation. And she would, at the same time, sharpen their ear for descriptive language.

"While I'm about it, I could read them short prose-poems by Ponge, the French poet. He writes about all sorts of things: a match, a telephone. His poems have such titles as "Butterfly," "Oyster," "Parisian." And I can also read them a few poems by Jules Laforgue. He's one of my favorite writers," she said.

The next day, Miss Bishop arrived in class carrying a shopping bag. She spread a newspaper on the classroom table and started taking things out of the bag: an egg beater, a white canvas shoe, two small potatoes, a fork, a knife, a spoon, and, finally, a packet of seeds. She arranged them carefully on the table, somewhat like a still life. "Now, I want you to write poems about these objects," she announced. "For that matter, I'll try my hand at it too."

I SAT NEXT TO STUDENTS Henry Carlile and Sandra McPherson that quarter. Henry, both as a young poet and friend, was serious, reflective, and entirely without affectations. And Sandy, even as a student, wrote poems that were well crafted and distinctive. Miss Bishop was impressed with them both. She said, over coffee, "Sandra McPherson already shows signs of becoming an interesting poet. What I like about her work is that she uses exactly her own materials. Some of my other students seem so reluctant to write about the things around them." Student Michael O'Conner's enthusiasm for poetry delighted her as well. "He has the nicest way of addressing me when he says 'Miss Bishop.' It's almost affectionate! His class poem yesterday had a line in it which I thought was actually rather good . . . the one about 'the kingdom of kiss.' I think Mr. O'Conner may know a bit about such matters, too. He's certainly charming enough. I imagine he's rather popular with the girls. Oh, those Irishmen! It must be something in their genes!"

The fact of the matter was that even though Miss Bishop felt herself to be an inexperienced and inept teacher, several of her students were already coming into their own under her watchful eye.

English poet Henry Reed became Elizabeth's closest literary friend in Seattle. While she was briefly in the hospital, Henry took over her classes. In his sonorous British accent he read Elizabeth's poems—which she had firmly refused to do—to her students. In the evenings Elizabeth and Henry were constantly on the telephone to each other, mostly comparing their frustrations in trying to teach poetry. They also went on a diet together. They dutifully got copies of an armed forces physical conditioning booklet. Henry would ask, "Well, Elizabeth, did you do your sit-ups today?"

"Did you do yours?"

I don't think this regimen lasted very long. Knowing Henry as I did, it couldn't have.

I ASKED HER, "Elizabeth, are you having to socialize much while you're here? Henry tells me that, as he puts it, 'going to faculty parties and giving poetry readings are all the go around here.'"

She responded by relating what had happened to her at such a gathering. "A man came up to me at a faculty party last night. He asked me what I would like to teach if I were to come back here again. Before I could stop myself, I said quite testily, 'Remedial reading!' I shouldn't have behaved that way. He was only trying to be cordial. But sometimes the level of literacy in my class appalls me. I wonder if some of my students have ever so much as looked at a dictionary, or if they would recognize one if they saw it. I think they simply guess at how to spell words. But I must say, the results can be quite original.

"I found out the other day, to my horror, that they don't even know the difference between a colon and a semicolon! Some of them speak so badly that I can't tell whether they're dumb or it's some kind of speech affectation. They keep saying things like, 'Oh, Miss Bishop, you *know* how it is.' And I'll say, 'No, I *don't* know how it is! Why don't you tell me how it is. I'm not a mind reader.'

"I asked them if any of them possibly knew what was wrong with that *ghastly* slogan: Winstons Taste Good, Like a Cigarette Should! There was complete silence in the classroom. I finally had to get out my *Dictionary of English Usage* and slowly read to them the definitions of *like* and *as*. When I got through, most of them were staring blankly at me. I could have walked right out at that point. But I said, 'If you students want so badly to *express* yourselves, why don't you bother to learn even the simplest things about your own language?' You studied with him—what did Theodore Roethke do about this sort of thing? What was I brought here to teach anyway!"

She looked at me in sheer exasperation, and I knew better than to attempt an answer or even venture a comment. She had more to say. "I wish my students wouldn't spend so much time trying to 'discover' themselves. They should let *other* people discover them. They keep telling me that they want to convey the Truth in their poems. The fact is that we always tell the truth about ourselves despite ourselves. It's just that quite often we don't like how it comes out. If my students would concentrate more on all the difficulties of writing a good poem, all the complexities of language and form, I think that they would find that the Truth will come through quite by itself.

"I *always* tell the truth in my poems. With 'The Fish,' that's *exactly* how it happened. It was in Key West, and I *did* catch it just as the poem says. That was in 1938. Oh, but I did change *one* thing: the poem says he had five hooks hanging from his mouth, but actually he had only three. I think it improved the poem when I made that change. Sometimes a poem makes its own demands. But I always *try* to stick as much as possible to what really happened when I describe something in a poem."

TOM ROBBINS, the writer, called Elizabeth to ask if he might interview her for *Seattle* magazine. Since she had just arrived in Seattle and didn't yet have a clear impression of its literary climate, she was somewhat nervous about such a discussion. She asked our mutual friend Gary Lundell and me to sit in on the interview the next evening. Gary and I arrived first at Elizabeth's apartment on Brooklyn Avenue, and Tom Robbins arrived a few minutes later.

"Miss Bishop," he asked her. "Would you like for your poetry to reach a wider audience?"

Elizabeth was momentarily puzzled by the question. She was perhaps a little suspicious of its possible implications. "Reach a *wider* audience? Now what would *that* mean?" She paused, and then continued, half to herself, "Well—I suppose it *might* mean that more of my books would *sell*. And that, of course, would mean more royalties for me. Yes! Now that you mention it, I suppose that I would like my work to, as you put it, reach a wider audience." She smiled, then added. "It's not that I like money for its own sake. Not at all. It's just that I can think of so many things I could *do* with it. More travel. I've always wanted to go to the Galapagos Islands. And, of course, I could buy still more books! Yes, come to think of it, that would be very nice." She gave him a sharp look. "Is that what you meant by your question? Or did you mean, do I crave vast popularity? If you did, then I'd have to answer: No, not especially."

ELIZABETH WAS NOT THE SORT of person to boast of a prize, though she had received many honors over the years. One evening, after I had spent an entire day with her, I learned from Dorothee Bowie that Elizabeth had received word just that morning of a major award. She had not even mentioned this to me. I telephoned her. "Elizabeth, you didn't tell me today about your fellowship. Why?"

"We were having such a nice time together that it entirely slipped my mind," she replied.

What I liked very much about Elizabeth was her restraint. You might even call it one-undermanship. She would never say she had "won" anything. Instead she might say, "I was given an award the other day. I don't know if I really deserved it, but having the money that comes with it will be very nice."

HER VIGNETTES OF FRIENDS were vivid little gems. I had spent the afternoon at the zoo with painter Jay Steensma, sketching and just walking about. Knowing how fond of animals Elizabeth was, I mentioned the visit to her. "Did I ever tell you," she asked, "about the time that Marianne Moore and her brother were returning from a family funeral? It had been a very sad day for them. They were driving home, not saying much to each other. Suddenly, looming up ahead of them on the highway was a sign for a roadside zoo. Oh, I'm sure you're familiar with the kind of zoo I mean. It will usually have some deer and goats, and perhaps even a bear or two.

"As you well know, Miss Moore loved animals and went to the zoo every chance she had. Her brother must have understood her very well. Perhaps he spotted Miss Moore looking longingly out the car window at the zoo sign. Before she could say anything, he said very firmly to her, 'No. No, Marianne, *Not today!*'"

ELIZABETH, GARY LUNDELL, mutual friend Jean Russell, and I spent a pleasant afternoon visiting sculptor Phillip McCracken and his wife, Anne, on Guemes Island. We also took Elizabeth to meet painter Guy Anderson in nearby La Conner. Guy invited us to join him and his close friend Deryl Walls for a drink at the Lighthouse Restaurant bar, across the street from his studio. It was so loud in there that Elizabeth and Guy couldn't have conversed even if they had tried to do so. They barely spoke to each other. There we all sat, suffering through our drinks. Maybe because Guy is very shy he had arranged it that way. In the car later, Elizabeth said, "Wes, did you notice that young fisherman, the boy who sat next to me? God knows what kind of mother complex he has. He spent the whole time sitting with his hand on my knee. I just ignored him, of course!"

ELIZABETH WAS NEVER so caught up in herself or in the distractions of the moment that it interfered with her judgment as a poet. I once watched her having drinks with a young poet at Lee's Restaurant. They were both drinking boisterously. I don't think the young poet was nearly as drunk as he may have been pretending to be. Knowing him as I did, I presumed to read his mind: "Miss Bishop seems to be a bit drunk. Aha! Maybe I can show her my poem now. If I show it to her when she's sober, I know she'll be much more critical."

The poet handed Elizabeth a poem he had just written. Elizabeth, wobbly though she was, read it carefully. "This is a ghastly poem!" she exclaimed.

The young poet was embarrassed. He had underestimated Elizabeth's unwavering acuity.

Elizabeth sized up the situation quickly. "I may be a little drunk, but I am *never* so drunk that I can't recognize a bad poem when I see it!"

SHE BROOKED NO NONSENSE when it came to the reading and writing of poetry. I still find it refreshingly abrasive simply to re-read, from time to time, the notes I took in her classes.

EB (first day of class, 5 January 1966): "I've gone through the poems which you handed in to me, and I've never seen so many haikus in my life, and they're not very well written either. They're more like the sort of thing one might jot down when one is feeling vaguely 'poetic.'

"And as for your rhymed poems — some of your rhymes are simply awful! We have to do some talking about the subtleties of rhyme well used.

"And you seem to write a lot of free verse out here. I guess that's what you call it. I was rather appalled. I just couldn't scan your free verse, and one *can* scan Eliot. I think some of you are misled about free verse. It isn't lined prose, and it isn't that easy. Look at Eliot. You can scan his descriptive poem "Cape Ann," for example, perfectly. And the same goes for *The Four Quartets* and *The Wasteland*. 'Under the firelight, under the brush, her hair / Spread out in fiery points / Glowed into words, then would be savagely still. . . .' You see, you'd never take this for prose. It's good free verse. Look also at E. E. Cummings — one can scan them — and the rain poems of Apollinaire. But these poems of yours are splattered all over the page, and I don't see any reason for it. I guess I'm rather old-fashioned.

"I'm going to have to be very strict with you, I see. For your first assignment, try to write something like A. E. Housman. I want something very *neat* — like a hymn. Some of you have a good ear: I think it's a gift from God. But your sense of rhyme and form is atrocious. I'm going to give you some strict meter assignments, and later on we'll do something with iambic pentameter.

"I would suggest you start by reading one poet — *all* of his poems, his letters, his biographies — everything *but* the criticisms on him. You should have your heads filled with poems all the time — poems by others, poems of your own making, poems you're still working on — until they almost get in your way," she told us. "I believe in the fortunate accident, but you don't sit down and try to have one. You have to be on the road before you can have an accident.

"A poet can't write poetry *all* the time, of course. So when he isn't writing, there are various other things he can do — dissipating, or inventing theories about poetry, or writing his memoirs. It comes to about the same thing.

"People seem to think that doing something like writing a poem makes one happier in life. Well, it doesn't solve anything. Perhaps it does give one the satisfaction of having done a thing well, or having put in a good day's work.

"There's an old Spanish proverb: A donkey who goes traveling comes back still a donkey."

EB (to the class, a few sessions later): "Everyone in this class likes Shakespeare, and after that, Dylan Thomas. But what about the seventeenth, and eighteenth century poets? And the nineteenth century? I was shocked yesterday when you didn't spot those quotations from Keats, Tennyson, and Swinburne. We had a whole year of Wordsworth, Keats, and Shelley when I was in high school. The Romantics are still awfully good poets. You *should* like Wordsworth. You're Nature people out here, and I'd expect you to like him.

"Have you read John Keats's letters? I recommend them highly. I think I enjoy them more than his poetry. He had a wonderful brain and a very strong character. Also, you should read Gerard Manley Hopkins's letters to Robert Bridges. They contain some of the best statements I've ever read about rhythm, meter, the writing of poetry. His journals, for sheer observation, are superb. He and Marianne Moore are the finest observers I've ever read.

"You should use more objects in your poems — observed images, those things you use every day, the things around you. Pop Art has brought so many *things* to our attention, whether we like them or not. One can write very good poetry without vivid images, but I myself prefer observation. . . . There are so many things you students are not taking advantage of — alliteration, internal rhyme.

"Let's try something. My view from the fourteenth floor of the Meany Hotel depresses me. I want you to write a poem, maybe thirty lines long, about Seattle. Here's a list of words to work in: viaduct, Space Needle, sea gull, cedar trees, Scenic Drive sign, cars. And I'll give a special prize to whichever one of you manages to come up with the best rhyme for Seattle."

ELIZABETH SOMETIMES wanted to discuss her students with me.

"All those students in my class — with their trusting eyes and their clear complexions," she sighed. "Have you seen the expensive cars that some of them drive? I don't know where they get their money; perhaps their parents help them out. Most of them look quite well fed and rather well off. And what do they write about in their poems? *Suffering,* of all things! I don't think most of them know *anything* about suffering, but their poems are just filled with it. I finally told them that they should come to Brazil and see for themselves what *real* suffering is. Then perhaps they wouldn't write so 'poetically' about it.

"I hardly know any of them, but I've already started worrying about some of my students. Going insane is very popular these days, and it frightens me to see so many young people flirting with the idea of it. They think that going crazy will turn them into better poets. That's just not true at all! Insanity is a terrible thing — *a terrible thing*! I've seen it first hand in some of my friends, and it is *not* the poetic sort of state that these young people seem to think it is. John Clare, that brilliant, *brilliant* nineteenth-century poet, did not write glorious poetry while he was in the asylum, I'm glad to say.

"Or they seem to think they should pursue an outrageous, helter-skelter sort of life — that sort of thing can become an end in itself. I've known Marianne Moore extremely well over a long time. Perhaps I'll tell my students about her sometime — to show them what variety, what startling depth and power can be drawn from such a relatively limited life.

"I think it's important that my students start to know some of these things. They have such narrow and sometimes destructive ideas about what it is to be a poet. I've been thinking lately that I really should say something to them about all of this. It's a very serious matter.

"And not everyone who writes well will be published. It's not a given. I've been fortunate from the start, winning prizes, having encouragement. Not that I've necessarily believed I've deserved it, but it's happened that way. Sometimes I don't feel that I'm an especially good poet, but when I read some of the things that some of my contemporaries are writing, I guess I'm not so bad after all.

"I've had only one rejection of a poem in my life. Somehow I always knew which poem to send to which magazine. But some of my students keep sending their poems to the most awful little poetry magazines. They seem to want so badly to be published that they don't care where. I told them the other day that they shouldn't waste their time sending their poems to the bad little poetry journals. They should aim for the best ones. Some of these little magazines can be rather good at times, but so many of them will publish just about anything that's sent to them."

ONE AFTERNOON Elizabeth had looked over my shoulder at one or two of my drawings. Her interest and her critical eye had been just what I'd needed at the moment, and we fell to discussing every artist's need for some sort of interaction with fellow artists. Elizabeth said to me: "I've never been one of those poets who will write a poem and then dash around showing it to everyone — pretending that they want criticism. Most of the times — in recent years anyway — I've usually known what's wrong with the poem. If I've shown my work to anyone for criticism, it's been to Cal [Robert] Lowell or Miss Moore. Cal likes my new poem, the one I call 'Poem.' He says it's very good. You can imagine how happy that makes me!"

"ELIZABETH, DO YOU EVER lose your motivation?" I once asked her.

"Lose my motivation? You ask me the oddest questions. Let me put it this way. I would say that sometimes my 'motivation' will come *back* for a day, maybe even for *two* days. And then I really have to get down to work. That happened to me a few weeks ago. I suddenly felt very 'motivated,' as you call it. I cleaned the kitchen oven and finally answered some letters. Is that what you mean about being motivated?" She smiled, then grew serious. "Or did you mean do I have sudden fits of inspiration to write poems? Oh, I hope you didn't mean something like that! I haven't been able to write a single good line in Seattle. Once or twice most of a poem has come to me all at once, but usually I write very, very slowly."

THERE WERE TIMES when Elizabeth Bishop was simply paralyzed by indecision. Her helplessness, whether it was justified or not, could leave her at an impasse just as decisions had to be made. Elizabeth often needed someone who could take charge at such times.

"Because I write the kind of poetry that I do, people seem to assume that I'm a *calm* person. Sometimes they even tell me how *sane* I am. But I'm not a calm person at all. I can understand how they might think that I am, but if they really knew me at all, they'd see that there are times when I can be as confused and indecisive as anyone. There are times when I really start to wonder what holds me together — awful times. But I feel a responsibility, while I'm here at least, to *appear* calm and collected — so these young people won't think that *all* poets are erratic."

"DID YOU READ what that young interviewer wrote about me? What was his name? — oh yes, Tom Robbins. He described me as looking and acting like some schoolmarm. That really hurt my feelings a bit. I used to be quite a tomboy. I was very good at climbing trees, and I did all sorts of wild things. And then they wanted a photograph of me to accompany the magazine interview. I *hate* being photographed. The only photograph I rather like is one where I'm lying on a bear rug going Goo! Goo! at the camera. That one I don't mind at all. I'm just not photographic, and never have been."

"SOME OF OUR CRITICS can find something in common between just about anything. Comparing me to Wittgenstein! I've never even read him. I don't know *anything* about his philosophy. Have you read Ernst Gombrich's *Art and Illusion?* He says all art comes from art. My own favorite reading is Darwin."

"I'M JUST BACK from giving a poetry reading in the Southwest. I didn't want to do it at all, but they do pay rather well down there. When I finished reading the first poem, the audience clapped so enthusiastically. I read another poem and they clapped even louder. I began to feel like some singer—like Judy Garland. All that applause! They really seemed to be enjoying it, and, to my dismay, I started to enjoy it myself. I'm afraid I may have a bit of the ham in me— more than I realized. Oh, I hope this isn't a bad sign."

"I HAD SOME PSYCHIATRY once—when it was fashionable to do that sort of thing, and some friends of mine had told me to try it. It didn't help me to understand myself any better, but it certainly helped me to understand some of my friends."

I ASKED ELIZABETH, "Do I have too many defenses?"
    "Too *many*? Can one ever have *enough* defenses?" she re-

plied. "One evening I was walking down Lexington Avenue, feeling bored and perhaps even a bit sorry for myself. I hadn't seen anyone for days, and no one had telephoned me. The only mail I'd received had been a few bills and circulars. I'd just had to get out of my apartment for a while. Then, of all things, I ran into Virgil Thomson. He was out for a walk—looking every bit as bored and down in the dumps as I was. Somehow that snapped me right out of it. The very thought that someone as brilliant and famous as Virgil Thomson could look so bored and at loose ends too quite cheered me up."

WHEN I HAD romantic problems, I liked to ask a variety of people for advice. Elizabeth was fixing me a sandwich one day. We were going to go shopping after a bite of lunch.

"Elizabeth, I need to ask you for some advice about love." She came to the kitchen doorway and stared incredulously at me.

"You want to ask me a question about w-h-a-t? Did you say it was about *love*? What could ever *possibly* give you the idea that I of *all* people would know *anything* about a thing like *that*!" she said. "If you ever were to know much about my personal life, you certainly wouldn't come to *me* for any sagely advice about a thing like love. I've usually been as confused about it as just about anyone else I've known. If you really are concerned about that subject, I'd suggest you go and read W. H. Auden. If *he* doesn't know something about love, I just don't know who else does."

Late that afternoon, after we had finished our shopping and were walking down University Way, she stopped and turned to me.

"Wes, I'm awfully sorry that I dodged your question the

way I did. It took me by surprise, and I didn't know how I should answer you. But I've been thinking about it, since you did ask me. And I will say *this* much: if any happiness ever comes your way, GRAB IT!"

WHEN I ARRIVED one evening at Elizabeth's small apartment on Brooklyn Avenue, the strains of a Brazilian samba filled the air. But I noticed how sad she looked. Was anything wrong, I asked?

"Yes. I'm homesick for Brazil," she said plaintively. "It's carnival time in Rio. If I were there now, I'd be lost in the crowds, dancing, staying up all night. The costumes are so imaginative! The music is simply wonderful. And another reason I'm so homesick for Brazil is that down there everyone is so *affectionate*! We go around all the time embracing one another. It's really very nice. We call it *abrango* — an embrace. Up here everyone shakes hands ever so properly. I just haven't adjusted to all this formality," she explained, adding, "Wes, when you leave this evening, would you do me a big favor? Would you mind giving me a hug instead of just another handshake? I wouldn't feel nearly so homesick if you did!"

I was flustered, but very pleased. I had wanted to give her a hug, but I had feared it wouldn't be at all appropriate.

AFTER ELIZABETH MOVED to Boston (she taught at Harvard from 1969 till 1977), I was out of touch with her for several months. Finally I telephoned her apartment at Lewis Wharf.

"Where *have* you been?" she demanded. "I haven't heard from you for so long. I haven't had a letter from you in *ages*! *Why*?"

"You're becoming so famous these days," I explained. "I just assumed everyone would be chasing after you day and night. I didn't want to write you a lot of letters you might feel you had to answer."

"I don't know *what* you're talking about! When the phone rang, I was walking in the door from having been at a tenants' meeting at Lewis Wharf—just to give you an example of how exciting my life here is. I can assure you I don't have fans pounding on my door around the clock or stalking me in the streets. Now please stop being so complicated," she said, "and just start writing me more letters."

She paused. "Actually, there is some rather exciting news. Octavio Paz and his wife have just been here from Mexico City. I'm awfully fond of the two of them. They much admired your paintings, by the way. We went up to Vermont for a few days, playing tourist. But while we were there, Octavio came down with a bad case of the flu."

"Oh, you mean he got a bad case of Robert Frost's revenge?"

"I'm going to pretend I didn't even hear that remark!" she answered, quickly changing the subject.

SHE NEVER STOPPED trying to improve my mind. Poet Léonie Adams had come to teach for a year at the University of Washington in 1969. "Léonie Adams is very serious. I think she may feel that I'm rather frivolous. Do go to her class. She'll have good things to say. She's very intelligent and is someone you would do well to listen to. She knows what she's talking about."

I HAD BEEN READING one of poet May Sarton's recently published diaries, but I hesitated to tell Elizabeth to whom I was referring.

"I've been trying to read some of the 'confessional poets' lately."

"Don't you have anything better to read than that? I'm really quite surprised at you. I *hate* confessional poetry, and so many people are writing it these days. Besides, they seldom have anything interesting to confess anyway. Mostly they write about a lot of things which I should think were best left unsaid. Dear, now you've got me a bit worried about your tastes in reading matter. Maybe I'd better send you some old copies of the *National Geographic*," she replied.

AND I HAVE MY OWN CONFESSION to make. What Elizabeth had, in fact, said to me was, "Maybe I'd better send you some travel books." But I took a deep breath when I transcribed this in 1979—and I changed her actual words. The reference to the *National Geographic* seemed somehow more Elizabethan to me, more like what she *might* have said. Some years later, I sent my notes to historian Solomon Katz to read. When he wrote back, he singled out the phrase "some old copies of the *National Geographic*" as being vintage Elizabeth Bishop! I promptly wrote to him, confessing my quotational sins.

SINCE I OFTEN DONATE LETTERS and manuscripts to various archives, I began to wonder how Elizabeth would take to my someday donating the letters she had written to me.

"Elizabeth, I need to ask you about what I should do eventually with the letters you've sent me. Would it be all right for me to donate them to some library or archive? They could be restricted, of course."

"Don't give them to any library—that would be sentimental. You should sell them instead—and ask a good price for them, if you can get it. You may need the money some day, and then you'd regret having given them away," she said. "That reminds me—a while ago I was in a little bookshop in Greenwich Village. There was a book I wanted to buy, but I didn't have enough money on me. So I asked the proprietor if I could make out a check. When he looked at the check, he asked me if I were Elizabeth Bishop the *poet*. I said yes. He said, 'Miss Bishop, I've been making some money off of you lately. I've just sold one of your letters for $100. It was a short one—typed, and with a handwritten postscript. And I sold another letter of yours for $125 not long ago.' Well! I had been writing and mailing letters most of that morning, and I had no idea they were so valuable. But I don't understand, Wes, why you think they should be restricted. I can pretty well remember what I've written to you, and I don't recall anything that should be restricted."

"Well, for instance," I replied, "in one of your letters you said, 'Another book by R——. The thought of it makes me shudder!'"

"I certainly would stand by that remark. You don't have to be so protective of me," she insisted. "Was there anything else I wrote that concerns you?"

"You called Sam F. an idiot."

"But he *is* an idiot!"

SEVERAL WEEKS BEFORE SHE DIED in 1979, I telephoned Elizabeth in Boston. During our conversation, I mentioned that, in addition to my class notes, I had taken notes over the years on some of her comments to me. I read her a few.

"They sound like things I might have said," she responded, "but I don't remember having said some of them. I'm glad you wrote them down. Some of those remarks are actually rather good! Would you mind sending me a copy? If someday I run out of things to say, I just may start quoting myself."

Elizabeth Bishop & Susanne Langer: A Conversation on University Way

ELIZABETH BISHOP WAS TO MEET philosopher Susanne K. Langer for the first time. It was 1966 and both of them were in Seattle. The three of us would have dinner together. As we walked toward the restaurant on University Way to join Dr. Langer, Elizabeth was edgy.

"I'm very nervous about meeting with Dr. Langer today. I don't have *any* background in philosophy. I won't know what to say to her," she said.

She was silent for a moment, and then she perked up.

"I *did* know John Dewey at Key West when he was quite old. One day he came up to me holding the prettiest little kitten. He was just fascinated by it. He showed it to me and said: 'Elizabeth, is there *anything* more beautiful than a cat's face?' And then, another time, he came up to me with a flower cupped in his hands. I liked him very much."

We went into the restaurant. After I had introduced them, Elizabeth and Dr. Langer exchanged a few amenities and settled down to ordering lunch. Dr. Langer turned to Elizabeth.

"Miss Bishop, tell me now. Are you enjoying teaching poetry?"

"I wish I could say that I am, but actually I'm finding it something of an ordeal. There's so much ground to cover, and in such a short time."

"I know exactly what you're talking about. It *is* frustrating having a class full of students. You're supposed to cram so much into their heads. And to make matters even worse, you're told that it has to be done within an academic quarter system."

"I didn't realize that you'd been a teacher."

"Oh, yes, indeed. I've put in my years at it. But now, thanks to Edgar Kaufmann, I can concentrate on my own work. Edgar's most generously given me a grant which frees me from having to teach."

"I have a little bit of financial independence myself. Some income which I inherited. Not a great deal. But enough to be a help," Elizabeth responded.

THE CONVERSATION LAPSED while we ate our lunches. Dr. Langer looked up suddenly, after having been somewhat pensive, and asked Elizabeth, "Are you a *patient* teacher, Miss Bishop? When I was teaching, some of my students were quite industrious. On the other hand, some of them could be impossibly lazy, and I'd completely lose patience with them. Do you have that sort of problem?"

"Oh yes," she sighed, "and not just with my students. Someone came up to me several evenings ago at a small

Susanne K. Langer and Wes Wehr at San Gregorio beach, San Francisco, 1968. Langer had given a lecture on the Berkeley campus the previous evening. Now it was time for a day of beachcombing (Photograph by Ralph Kennedy)

gathering here — one of those faculty parties teachers so often feel they have to give. He asked me what I would like to teach if I were to come back here again. I was irritable and tired from an especially ghastly day in class. I answered him rather nastily in the negative. I must have startled the poor man. He looked quite confused and made a very quick exit. I shouldn't, I suppose, have snapped at him that way."

"Well, as a matter of fact," said Dr. Langer, smiling, "I'm rather glad to hear that. I'm glad to know that I'm not the *only* short-tempered teacher around. Some of my colleagues are the souls of patience with their students and friends. But I'm always sticking my foot in my mouth."

Elizabeth was surprised. "*You?* I can't imagine that!"

"Oh, it's quite true, I can assure you," responded Dr. Langer. "Sometimes someone or other will start telling me something, even lecturing me. And, more often than not, I'll be about ten jumps ahead of him. I can often anticipate what direction an argument is going to take, or someone else's train of thought. Quite often I'll know just about what they're going to say next, sometimes even before they do. I'm not the most patient sort of person. I'll quite forget my good manners and cut people right off in the middle of a sentence. You can imagine how popular that makes me in some quarters."

Elizabeth shot a glance at me. She was obviously enjoying Dr. Langer's candor.

"Of course," she added, "I do have some colleagues who can keep me hanging on their every word. Jerome Bruner, the psychologist, for instance. I have great respect for him. But the people I would most want to hash out my ideas with are usually so busy with their own work, and I with mine, that we just don't get to see much of each other. And I sorely regret that."

"I gather, from what you say, that you don't lead a particularly gregarious life," Elizabeth commented.

"Hardly. I lead a quite secluded life. Partly I leave it up to our mutual friend Wes, here, and his almost daily letters to keep me posted on at least some of what's going on. I have to be a social porcupine if I'm ever going to finish my book. After the house chores and all the other stuff one always has to attend to, there simply isn't much time left over for socializing." She suddenly asked Elizabeth, "I've written some poems myself, but I'm hardly what anyone would call a professional poet. Do any of your poems come easily and quickly?"

"Oh, no. I write very slowly."

"I'm the same way. Often, with my philosophical work, I will write out a manuscript, put it away, take it out months later, reread it, put it away again. I keep doing this until I can see the weaknesses in it, or that it's simply no good and has to be chucked out. It often happens with me that I have to start all over again from scratch."

"There are other poets who seem to be able to write good poems much more readily than I ever can," said Elizabeth.

"And there are some philosophers like that, too. Bertrand Russell could write something right off, and it would be *good*. I have to revise incessantly. You really should see some of my manuscripts and galley proofs with all their cross-outs and paste-overs."

THE DINNER LASTED about an hour and a half. Later that evening I visited Dr. Langer.

"I certainly enjoyed meeting Miss Bishop today. She is a good poet, a very good poet. It's a pity we live so far apart. She's someone I certainly would welcome seeing again. I'm leaving for Old Lyme tomorrow and probably won't see her again. When you talk with her next, would you please tell her for me what a real pleasure it was for me to have some time with her today," she said.

SEVERAL DAYS LATER, I relayed the message to Elizabeth. She looked both pleased and skeptical.

"Now, Wes. Be *honest* with me. Did Dr. Langer really say those nice things, or are you just trying to be polite? She's a remarkable woman, and I'm really surprised that she should have read any of my poetry, let alone have said such nice things about it. I've heard about how you like to play Cupid with some people, so I think I'd just better take it with a grain of salt."

Léonie Adams
in Seattle

POETS WHO CAME TO TEACH at the University of Washington during the 1950s and 1960s routinely arrived in January, the worst possible month of the year. For visiting teacher-poets such as Elizabeth Bishop, Léonie Adams, Henry Reed, Richard Eberhart, Rolfe Humphries, and Galway Kinnell, their first impressions of Seattle were of a relentlessly rainy city of short winter days and long, dark nights. The pay offered for teaching poetry could be enticing, but the personal price must sometimes have seemed high. Other poets who gave readings in Seattle and visited here briefly—William Carlos Williams, Dylan Thomas, Alan Ginsberg, Robert Lowell, and Robert Penn Warren, to name a few—declared the weather dismal.

It was January 1969. Léonie Adams had just arrived,

to be greeted by an unusually heavy snowfall which had left the campus and nearby streets blanketed with snow and slush. She was not in good health, so English department secretary Dorothee Bowie suggested I check in on Miss Adams. I expected fragility. I couldn't have been more wrong. I knocked on her door at the Wilsonian Hotel and was greeted by a woman whose lively, direct, no-nonsense gaze and strong contralto voice conveyed her singular vitality. I introduced myself, dropped a few names of mutual poet friends, and asked if I might run any errands for her. Thereafter, almost before I knew it, Miss Adams and I were having lunch and dinner together regularly. We nearly always dined at Lee's Restaurant on University Way.

Theodore Roethke had taught poetry at the University of Washington from 1948 until his death in 1963. Miss Adams was now to teach some of Roethke's classes. She wanted to know which poets Roethke had taught while I studied with him. I mentioned a long list of poets, including William Butler Yeats, Gerard Manley Hopkins, John Donne, Dylan Thomas, Wallace Stevens, Marianne Moore, Louise Bogan, and Miss Adams. I also mentioned Roethke's inclusion of Hart Crane's poetry.

"Have you read Hart Crane's *Voyages?*" she asked.

"I certainly have," I replied. "We spent a good part of one quarter reading Crane's poems, and his letters too. I was so dazzled by the *Voyages* that I didn't have to try to memorize them. There are whole passages you just don't forget once you've read them. Why did you ask?"

"A man I just saw in the street outside the restaurant window reminded me that I once knew the man who inspired the

Three "Ash Can Cats": Léonie Adams, Margaret Mead, and Eleanor Pelham Kortheuer during their undergraduate days at Vassar College (Photograph from the collections of the Library of Congress)

Voyages," she said. "His name was Emil. He knew a lot about the sea and faraway places. He had been a merchant seaman. He was pleasant and somewhat conventional, likeable in his way. But he wasn't an especially exciting man. Not by any means. He did, however, inspire Hart to write some magnificent poetry. When Emil finally read Hart's Voyages, I remember how upset he was when he realized that he was the central subject. He couldn't comprehend how Hart could have been so inspired by him. It embarrassed him a great deal. Hart had a wonderful imagination, and Emil must have recounted his experiences at sea in a truly vivid way. In any case, it certainly did ignite Hart's imagination and lead ultimately to some of the most exalted poetry in our time."

Her remarks struck a chord with me. I'd noted a similar fact about painters. "When I look at photographs," I said, "of some of the places in France that inspired Cezanne's great landscapes — or at photographs of some of the people who sat for his greatest portraits — how lackluster the actual landscapes and original models often seem when compared with Cezanne's depictions of them."

"That's my point," she went on to say. "It's quite interesting to see how the poet's imagination can seize upon ordinary experience, can transform and intensify it and raise it to such heights. Splendid poems can spring from a chance remark. Or from something one might casually notice along the street. Good poets really do have a special instinct for those moments that can become the seed of a poem. They don't have to go looking for things to write about. They recognize them when they appear, wherever

and however that may be. In a way, they're almost given
to the poet. Then the poet, in turn, has to give them their
form and rightness, or somehow find it," she commented,
adding, "I tell my students: Don't merely describe things. Let
them get at you. And, if you're lucky, they'll start to whis-
per some of their secrets to you. Don't impose too much of
yourself upon them. Let them reveal their own natures
to you. You have to develop a very keen ear to catch what
they will have to say. And then your poem's work is cut out
for you."

She gave me a piercing look. "As a painter, you should
already know this very well, Wes. A poem is like a still-
life painting. It isn't something that merely describes things,
or makes a list of them. The poet, and the painter, too, have
to somehow discover and reveal these secret connections —
how objects relate to each other in complex and mysterious ways. Look at these objects around us — that vase on the
cashier's counter with its garish plastic flowers, that crum-
pled napkin in the aisle, that wet umbrella in the corner.
These things may look like separate and ordinary objects,
but to the poet they may imply the most rich and unexpected metaphorical relationships. They're very much a
part of our lives, in far deeper ways than we realize. They're
emblems — symbols — of our values and attachments. A
true poet, a true artist has the gift — and the responsibility —
of looking and listening more deeply than most other
people do."

I sat listening to Léonie, remembering what Elizabeth
Bishop had told me: "Léonie Adams is very serious. I think
she may feel I'm rather frivolous. Do go to her class. She'll

have good things to say." And now, here was Léonie Adams, evoking for me the depths of a still-life by Chardin, or by the Italian painter Morandi. Here, unexpectedly, was a poet discussing the secrets of still-life painting.

This surprised me. Elizabeth Bishop was well known for her precision in observing and writing about objects. She was also a painter of charming, carefully observed scenes and objects. It was intriguing to me that Léonie Adams, whose poems were often more philosophical, more abstract, should talk about objects in much the same way that Bishop did. And I thought of those haunting, luminous lines from Adams's poem "Country Summer," realizing that her images worked so well, both as object and emblem, because of the absolute accuracy of her poet's eye:

Into the rooms flow meadow airs,
the warm farm baking smell's blown round
inside and out, and sky and ground
are much the same; the wishing star,
Hesperus, kind and early born,
is risen only finger-far;
All stars stand close in summer air,
and tremble, and look mild as amber;
when wicks are lighted in the chamber,
they are like stars which settled there.

Now straightening from the flowery hay,
down the still light the mowers look,
or turn, because their dreaming shook,
and they waked half to other days,
when left alone in the yellow stubble
the rusty-coated mare would graze.
Yet thick the lazy dreams are born,
another thought can come to mind,
but like the shivering of the wind,
morning and evening in the corn.

Gradually, Léonie Adams met more and more people at the usual English department literary functions. In our provincial eagerness to extol to her the cultural virtues of the Pacific Northwest, too many of us talked incessantly about Theodore Roethke, or about the painters Mark Tobey and Morris Graves. Finally, Léonie couldn't take any more of it.

"Wes," she snapped, "doesn't anyone around here talk about anyone besides Theodore Roethke, Mark Tobey, and Morris Graves? With all due respect for their very impressive accomplishments, I'm surprised by all this talk. After a while, I've had quite my fill of it. In New York, famous people are a commonplace. If one has to talk about them, at least there are more from whom to pick and choose!"

ONE EVENING, LÉONIE and I went to hear poet John Berryman. He had been invited to Seattle to read his poetry for the Roethke Memorial Reading on campus. Berryman was hamming it up, so much so that Léonie, drumming her fingers on the armrest of her seat, grew increasingly restless and out of patience with his antics. Finally, Berryman began to read from his recently completed *Dream Poems* sequences. The poems were magnificent. Léonie's ears pricked up; her eyes fixed intently upon Berryman. When he finished, Léonie sat bolt upright, a jubilant flash in her eyes. She turned to me.

"Well, *finally*! That's the *real* thing! It certainly took John long enough to get down to it. But it was well worth the wait! Just because he's way out here in Seattle is no excuse for him to put on all that swaggering floor show. I came here tonight to hear poetry, not to watch a ham actor!" she exclaimed.

I WAS A PUZZLEMENT to Léonie. It wasn't clear to her exactly what I did. I had told her about my taking poetry workshops from Roethke, Eberhart, and Bishop. I had mentioned to her that I had composed a lot of chamber music and had set many contemporary poems, including hers, to music. But mostly I seemed to be preoccupied with painting.

"If you started out as a composer, how did you become a painter?" she asked.

"I don't know. I haven't really thought about it. But I do suspect it has something to do with pats on my head. Maybe I've been the victim of compliments and approval. I received more compliments as a painter than I ever did as a composer. So much for my being dedicated!" I answered, almost randomly.

Léonie immediately thought of a similar instance. "That's just the way it can go. When Bill [Léonie's husband, critic William Troy] and I were living in Paris, James Joyce would come to our apartment. Bill and I quickly realized that James did not especially to want talk about writing. He wanted to play our piano and sing songs for us. Fortunately he had a very fine voice. Before he became a writer, his real ambition had been to be a professional singer. The turning point for him was when he entered a vocal contest in Ireland. Much to his disappointment, it was John McCormack who won the first prize. McCormack, of course, became a very popular singer later. If James Joyce had won that prize, it's possible that he would never have gone on to become a great writer. Yes, I can understand what you mean about approval playing a role in an artist's life," she said.

My schedule made it difficult for me to attend Léonie's poetry classes. Besides, I was having dinner with her almost nightly at Lee's Restaurant, and our dinner conversations, which often lasted until closing time, were interwoven with apt lines of poetry, her own or other's, lofty or lyrical, declaimed in her unforgettable voice. Out of the clear sky, she would lift her double-martini glass in a sort of toast, and an incisive and beautiful verse would follow, never the same one twice. These were incredible moments. She was always clear-headed, but she was intoxicated with poetry!

Since Léonie didn't say much about her classes, I finally made a point of asking her how they were going.

"Actually, quite well, thank you," she replied. "I rather like my students, but I'm being very careful not to praise them overmuch, even if one of them has done something exceptionally well. I've already found that overpraising can make them acutely self-conscious. They start worrying about what they should do next to solicit or earn more and higher praise from me. From then on this kind of distraction colors what they write and spoils everything! I tell them instead that I *like* something one of them has written, or that one of them has just said something quite *sensible*. I give them encouraging comments rather than extravagant praise. I'm convinced that this kind of moderation on my part is far better for them in the long run. For that matter, I personally don't mind compliments, but I don't like effusiveness, even if it's well intended."

I asked her if she had known any memorable teachers when she was a young student.

"Yes, I have," she said, with a smile. "Believe it or not, I too was a student once. You can imagine how long ago that was! I had a most interesting lady for a French teacher when I was very young. One day she stopped right in the middle of our French lesson and said to our class — 'Mes enfants, do you happen to know what is the tragic flaw in man? It is l'égoïsme, the ego, pride! And, my dears, do you know what is the tragic flaw in woman? It is the need to belong!' — oh, how often have I found that to be true!"

DURING THE 1920S, a now-legendary group of anthropologists and poets congregated at Barnard College in New York to study with the great anthropologist Franz Boas. Boas was then the most eminent and controversial anthropologist in America. The list of names of his students and colleagues now reads like the Who's Who of American anthropologists: Ruth Benedict, Edward Sapir, A. L. Kroeber, Margaret Mead, to name only a few. Two of my anthropology teachers at the University of Washington in 1949–1950 had been students of Franz Boas: Erna Gunther and Melvin Jacobs. At Alert Bay, British Columbia, in 1967, Gary Lundell and I had met several elder Kwakiutls who remembered Boas from his 1911 visits to Alert Bay. And now, to my surprise, I discovered that Léonie Adams had also studied with Franz Boas.

I became aware of this in a surprising way: I saw a Barnard College class-days photograph of the *Ash Can Cats* in an autobiography by Margaret Mead. The picture included both Léonie Adams and Margaret Mead as former classmates and roommates. In 1923, Léonie had been, she told me, a bridesmaid at Mead's first marriage. The friendship between Léonie Adams and Margaret Mead was a lasting and important one for both of them. In fact, according to Mead's biographer, Jane Howard, during the 1960s and seventies, when Mead got to an airport an hour before flight time, she would head for a phone booth and use the hour to talk with Léonie. "An hour," Mead would say, "is about the time it takes to catch up with Léonie!"

I had introduced Gary Lundell to Léonie. Gary was, as was I, intrigued by Léonie's background as part of the famed Boas circle. Later I told Léonie more about Gary. She liked his paintings and wanted to know more about him. "Gary and I were in Alert Bay for the raising of the Mungo Martin memorial pole," I told her. "We met several Kwakiutls who remembered Franz Boas and liked him very much. Did you actually study with Boas?," I asked.

"Yes, I did. Those were grand days! For one thing, Edward Sapir and Ruth Benedict were writing poetry. Louise Bogan and I were writing poetry. And Margaret [Mead] was even trying her hand at it! We all were writing poetry! I know the photograph you speak of very well. It's from when Margaret and I were rooming together at Barnard."

One evening, over dinner at Lee's Restaurant, Léonie told

me, "Margaret was on television two nights ago. I telephoned her the next day, and I said: 'Margaret, it's Léonie. I've just been listening to you on television, and you've gone too far again! You're a great anthropologist, but I just don't understand why you spoonfeed people. I know that you know better than to say some of the things you do. Is this what happens to people when they become celebrities? What would Boas think if he were here and heard you say some of those things? They're oversimplified, and you know it. I don't begrudge you your fame. That's not it at all. I just wish that it were based more on your best contributions and not so much on your colorful personality. I had to telephone you and speak my mind because I have too much respect for you. Now that I've got that out of my system, Margaret, tell me, how are you?'"

After Léonie had finished quoting herself to me, she contentedly buttered a roll. I wondered silently: Is this a case of compulsive frankness? Or unmitigated gall? Or admirable directness and honesty? Or just some kind of sour grapes? Sometimes the fine line between candor and rancor is hard to pinpoint. I couldn't decide. Besides, my task was to transcribe Léonie, not to try to interpret her. Whatever one might call it, I doubted that anybody else could have gotten away with lecturing Margaret Mead the way Léonie Adams did.

I NEVER ASKED Léonie outright how she felt about acclaim and recognition, but on one occasion, at least, I had an accidental glimpse into what kind of acknowledgment meant the most to her. Painter Morris Graves had just sent me a very enthusiastic letter from California. He had just seen a show of my new paintings at the Humboldt Galleries in San Francisco and had written me about it. Elizabeth Bishop had written what she called "the blurb" for the exhibition. Léonie read Morris Graves's letter carefully and handed it back to me, saying:

"When an artist receives a letter like this from an artist such as Morris Graves, all the rest is really nothing more than mere background noise. Something like this has happened to me twice. When Louise [Bogan] and I shared the Bollingen award, Wallace Stevens told a mutual friend of ours: 'I'm glad they gave it to Léonie. She deserves it!' The other time was when T. S. Eliot came to New York. There was a big party for him. All the important poets and hangers on were there. They all gathered around Mr. Eliot, toasting him. Finally, I heard later, he said to them: 'Thank you very much. You are all most kind. But where is Léonie Adams? I would very much like to meet her! I take my hat off to Léonie Adams!'

"I've had some recognition of different kinds since then, but it's all been background noise by comparison. And now you've had this beautiful letter from Morris Graves. As a painter, what more could you possibly wish for?"

FOR LÉONIE ADAMS, recognition could mean a few warm words of admiration from a poet whom she in turn admired—from Wallace Stevens and T. S. Eliot, for instance. For Elizabeth Bishop, besides how much it pleased her when Robert Lowell or Marianne Moore liked a new poem of hers, recognition could be equated with being able to afford a trip to the Galapagos Islands, or another book buying spree.

Elizabeth and Léonie had at least one thing in common; they were both superb poets. Apart from that, they were very different in several ways. When Elizabeth was caustic, her words were deft and left no room for a coherent response.

Her put-downs were memorably effective. Her exasperated words didn't so much blindly lash out and condemn as they calmly held up a mirror to the vanity, insecurities, and ludicrousness of anyone who offended her sense of good manners and protocol. Elizabeth often, however, seemed to be entirely helpless, genuinely so, nearly paralyzed by indecision. It was not a ploy for attention. Her helplessness could border on desperation. Then, her good friends appeared from all directions to protect her from her misfortunes, and from herself.

By contrast, Léonie never struck me as being helpless. There was a tacit self-reliance and a fiercely independent streak in her which I immediately recognized. Knowing that Léonie was almost daily walking in the snow from the Wilsonian Hotel to her classroom at the English department, I phoned Dorothee Bowie to ask what I should do. Dorothee answered: "Let Léonie do things her own way. She's a real pro, in the best sense of the word!" Dorothee was right. Any gestures on my part that might even appear to be solicitous would be resented. It was clear to me that what Léonie wanted was a kind of relaxed and respectful companionship, an attentive audience during our winter evening dinners on University Way. Léonie was well aware that people came forth from time to time to protect and help Elizabeth. I think she was even capable of resenting it a bit, but such resentment would have been short-lived, insignificant. Léonie respected Elizabeth far too much for it to be otherwise. Indeed, though Léonie was not close to Elizabeth, I think that any serious disrespect shown by anyone toward Elizabeth would have rankled if not angered Léonie. She would, I suspect, have taken it personally.

I KNOW THAT ELIZABETH respected and liked Léonie, even though their lives moved in different orbits much of the time.

Elizabeth asked me on the telephone, "Wes, are you seeing much of Léonie? I hope so. The poor dear is not having an easy time of it just now. I wish that there were something I could do to help. But Léonie has a proud streak. I have to remember that. Please do remember me to her. I'm very fond of her, probably more than she would guess."

SOME MUSICIANS
& AN ACTOR

Student Days: *Queen Anne High School & the University of Washington*

DURING THE SO-CALLED POST-DEPRESSION 1940s, money was scarce. My father ran a Texaco service station near Lake Union, in the downtown Seattle area. Because I seemed incapable of learning how to drive a car, let alone repairing and servicing one, it soon became clear I could not follow in my father's footsteps. I was by then already a student at Queen Anne High School, and my parents agreed that the time was ripe for practical training in a field I was more likely to master.

I studied piano with Mrs. Vance Thompson, a pleasant lady who came once a week to the Magnolia Bluff house where my parents and I lived. Mrs. Thompson taught the E. Robert Schmitz Piano Method—an approach to piano playing based on Schmitz's physiological analysis of hand and arm muscles. The terminology was daunting: "upper humeral rotation," "metacarpal articulation," "digital dexterity," and so on. I soon discovered a way to avoid both practicing the piano and having to learn all the mechanical ins and outs of the Schmitz piano system—I began to compose little piano pieces. When Mrs. Thompson arrived for the weekly lesson, she invariably found me unprepared. I had not practiced the piano pieces I was supposed to learn. I had instead spent the time composing. All I could show her, week after week, was a new piano composition. Being of a pragmatic nature, Mrs. Thompson saw the unlikelihood of her teaching me how to play the piano properly. She instead spent our "piano lessons" going over my newest piano piece.

My piano pieces often had a Spanish flavor. Or they were amorphous meanderings, with such titles as "Reverie in A minor," "Pastoral in B flat major," and "End of Summer in E flat major," making an occasional excursion into a different key. It was quite by accident that I had my first encounter with "modern" music. Sherman Clay, a music store in downtown Seattle, had a remarkably good selection of recordings of both classical and modern music. One afternoon in 1946 or so, I discovered recordings of Bela Bartok's *Piano Concerto No. 3* and Alban Berg's *Violin Concerto* on the music store shelves. These two works became my introduction to contemporary music. I went to the Seattle Public Library to check out the score of the Bartok concerto. One thing led to another, and a librarian showed me the music listening rooms. For several hours I sat transfixed, listening to recording after recording of music by Stravinsky, Bartok, Schönberg, Berg, Hindemith, and more modern composers than I can now recall.

For many years I had thought that music consisted

Mark Tobey, at his University District house, coaching musician-painter Windsor Utley and composer-pianist Lockrem Johnson in rehearsal of his original composition for flute, 1950 (Photograph courtesy of Seattle Times*)*

mainly of poetic little piano pieces written in the blandest of harmonies. By contrast, these "contemporary" composers made no sense to me, but my ears reveled in the strange, exciting rhythms and colorful harmonies of their music. After that experience, I couldn't go on writing watered-down Spanish dances or the occasional misguided "homage" to Beethoven, such as my thunderous piece for piano entitled "Napoleon's Retreat," in which I evoked, chord by chord, Napoleon's defeated and exhausted army in retreat across the blizzard-stricken, desolate steppes of Russia.

The most far out of the modern composers was Arnold Schönberg, who wrote music that wasn't in *any* musical key at all! Inspired by Schönberg's abstract music, I composed a piano piece entitled "Moment Morose." This piece consisted of about eight bars of murky, aimless chords. It seemed neither quite to begin nor clearly to end. I played it for Mrs. Thompson at my next lesson. When I finished she looked worried.

"Moment Morose" had only one public performance. When I played it for the Queen Anne High School class in assembly hall, the silence that followed my torturously expressive performance didn't daunt me a bit. I rose from the piano and bowed in several directions regardless. Several weeks later, I sent the clumsily annotated little manuscript to Arnold Schönberg himself in Beverly Hills. I was so blithely innocent and oblivious that it never occurred to me that Mr. Schönberg would suspect me of childish malice, which was not the case at all.

Mrs. Thompson pressed valiantly on, trying to teach me how to play the piano. Finally the time came when she needed to appeal to higher authority—her own teacher,

E. Robert Schmitz, the master himself. Mrs. Thompson suggested I attend his piano classes, along with the rest of her piano students, during his annual visit to Seattle. Schmitz had a private music conservatory in San Francisco where he taught piano when he wasn't traveling around the country giving piano concerts and conducting piano classes.

Schmitz was rather famous. In Paris he had founded the Association des Concerts Schmitz, assembling a full orchestra and chorus to perform French works. In 1918 he emigrated to the United States, where he performed with the Boston Symphony and the New York Philharmonic and played the music of contemporary composers in recital. In 1923 he organized Pro Musica, a group that brought numerous great modern European composers — including Ravel, Bartok, Milhaud, Respighi, and Prokofiev — to the United States to give concerts. Some of these visiting composers gave recitals in the Spanish Ballroom at Seattle's Olympic Hotel during the 1930s and 1940s. Schmitz had also been quick to realize the genius of American composer Charles Ives at a time when performances of Ives were few and far between.

New York Times music critic Virgil Thomson, the most influential and feared music critic of his time, could be demolishingly sarcastic and condescending in his reviews. Many of the most celebrated composers and performers of the 1940s and 1950s were given the critical axe by him. He had entitled his review of a performance by one famous violinist, "In Tune, but Not with the Infinite!" Thomson, however, singled out Schmitz's performance of Debussy's demonically difficult "Piano Etudes" as a highpoint in supreme pianism. For one thing, Thomson was a Francophile of the most militant sort.

Schmitz was well known in Seattle's musical circles long before I began to study with him. On January 21, 1921, Nellie C. Cornish, founder and director of the Cornish School, and a small group of her pupils watched ground being broken for the construction of the school at Harvard Avenue North and East Roy Street in Seattle. Miss Cornish was busy that year interviewing prospective teachers for the summer school. Among the candidates was Mr. Schmitz. His lectures on piano technique, according to Miss Cornish's autobiography, were given in various cities while he was en route to Seattle. This had led to a large enrollment of piano students at Cornish during 1921.

MY ANNUAL LESSONS with Schmitz were expensive. Twenty dollars an hour during the early 1940s was a lot of money. Somehow my parents put the money aside for these lessons. My mother's philosophy was that it was important I have at least an introduction to the kind of worldly background Schmitz brought to our piano classes and private lessons.

Schmitz was tall and thin, and even when he was serious, he had a lurking streak of playfulness. He was encouraging to me, almost fatherly. As I stumbled ineptly through Debussy's "Maid with the Flaxen Hair," he stopped me. "My boy," he said, "this is only a simple country girl. You have put peroxide in her hair. Please, play this passage very *simply*!" I suspect Schmitz was fond of this quip and had occasion to use it often.

I heard Schmitz perform in person only once — at the Moore Theater. The audience was moderately large, mainly because the piano teachers who propagated the Schmitz method locally had seen to it that their students and the students' parents had all bought tickets to this concert. I can't remember what he played that evening, let alone how well he played it. My attentions were elsewhere because I had attended the performance with a piano student named Barbara Boulton. I had a crush on her, and I wanted to impress her with how well I got on with Schmitz. I asked an usher friend to deliver a handwritten note to Schmitz backstage at intermission. "Dear Mr. Schmitz," it read, "I am here tonight with my girlfriend, Barbara Boulton. She is very nice. She plays the piano. Her favorite piano piece is 'Clair de lune.' Would you please play it for her as an encore? Thank you very much. Your student, Wesley Wehr."

At the end of the piano recital, Mr. Schmitz stepped to the footlights. He quickly spotted Barbara and me sitting conspicuously on the fifth or sixth row. "I have had a special request to play 'Clair de lune,' which I shall do with pleasure," he announced. Barbara was visibly thrilled. Shy as she was, she nevertheless kissed me quickly on the cheek. We sat through the remaining encores holding hands, trying to concentrate on Mr. Schmitz's dazzling technique at the piano.

ALTHOUGH SCHMITZ WAS A PIANIST and teacher, his concerts and master classes had an atmosphere one usually associates with religious events. Schmitz, although good natured and convivial, nevertheless maintained exactly the proper distance from his students and disciples. He was something of a counterpart to the theosophist lecturer and teacher Krishnamurti who was also based in California. They both had piercing eyes, resonant voices, and a certain persuasive parental authority.

Schmitz had rather liked the first piano piece I played for him: my "Spanish Dance No. 1 for piano solo." I must have had beginner's luck. He returned yearly to Seattle to conduct master classes and give private lessons. Each year, when I showed him my latest piano composition, he looked increasingly dismayed, even disenchanted. He finally took Mrs. Thompson aside after a lesson. "I don't understand," I heard him complaining to her. "Wesley is not getting any better; he's getting worse!" There was nothing surprising about that. I had the barest of musical gifts, and I was too lazy and undisciplined to develop even those minimal talents.

Each of my private lessons with Schmitz lasted exactly one hour. At the precise moment, an assistant watching the clock in the next room would knock on the door to announce the next student. My lessons were often taken up with Schmitz's anecdotes about the many composers he had known. I didn't learn much about playing the piano from him, but I did get a good introduction to a world of music that extended far beyond the confines of Seattle in the 1940s.

My final audition with Schmitz was dismal. I had composed two songs for voice and piano, "Lament" and "Low Tide," which singer June Beard and I performed in a student recital at Meany Hall on the University of Washington campus. The audience liked them. Several of the music faculty seemed surprised by them and were unusually enthusiastic. June and I took several curtain calls. With that sort of reception, I felt confident I could bring these songs to Schmitz. June and I arranged to meet him in the concert auditorium at the Fisher Studio building in downtown Seattle. When we finished performing the songs, Mr. Schmitz sat down beside me on the piano bench, greatly exasperated. "Hasn't

Violinist Bonnie Jean Douglas and composer Wes Wehr
rehearsing his sonata for violin and piano, 1952
(Photograph courtesy of Seattle Times)

anyone told you that parallel fifths are *forbidden*? Your counterpoint is impossible! Worse than that! It's nonexistent!"

June Beard had sung the songs magnificently. Her rich, soaring voice and flexible technique could transform any young composer's songs into a musical experience. But Mr. Schmitz said nothing at all to her. He was angrily preoccupied with telling me what an inept piece of music I had subjected him to. This was to be my last lesson with him. Shortly after that, Mrs. Thompson telephoned me to announce that Mr. Schmitz had died unexpectedly in San Francisco.

WHILE I WAS STILL ATTENDING Queen Anne High School in Seattle in 1946, my parents took me to the University of Washington Music Department to meet George Frederick McKay—"The Dean of Northwest Composers." McKay had taught a number of prominent composers, including Earl Robinson, composer of *Ballad for Americans*. McKay was well known for his choral music and orchestral pieces, some of which I had heard while I was still in high school. I liked his music very much.

I had composed a dozen or so piano pieces that exhibited more unbridaled theatricality than coherent craft. My all-purpose masterpiece was "Spanish Dance No. 1." If you listened carefully, you could hear just about every imaginable Spanish composer making a brief appearance in this slapdash piece of music. "Moment Morose" had bombed so badly when I performed it at Queen Anne High School that I was very cautious now about what I played in public.

McKay invited me to play my pieces for his music composition class. They listened good naturedly to my musical ramblings and poundings. When the class was over, he invited me to come back again any time. Since I was still in high school, I couldn't formally enroll in his classes. But when I had to decide which major to elect in college, I knew I wanted to study with George McKay.

MCKAY WAS TALL and somewhat lanky. He tended to talk softly, to the point of mumbling. An avowed humanist, he was the most "philosophical" member of the music faculty and was, all in all, a noble man. He was also something of a subversive presence in the Northwest musical scene. That is, he encouraged young composers to explore the musical riches of their own local and indigenous traditions and not slavishly to emulate the European old masters. He introduced us to Northwest Coast Native American music and to American folk music. His point was straightforward and historically accurate: the great European composers — Mozart, Haydn, Beethoven, Chopin, Schubert, Bartok, and Kódály, for instance — had been inspired by the folk and popular music of their own time and place. McKay's own music exemplified what he taught. It lacked pretentiousness of any kind.

It was not unusual for McKay to come up to his students in the music department hallway and abruptly ask: "Are you *really* satisfied with your objectives? Have you even thought about them very seriously? Are they what you *really* want out of life?"

Whenever I brought a new musical composition to McKay for criticism, he was usually easy on me, pointing out what he liked about the score. After several years of study with him, I brought him a movement for string quartet. He looked through the music, playing parts of it on the upright piano in his studio. He hummed parts of it to himself. Finally he closed the score. "This is rather nice," he said, "It moves along fairly well. It has a respectable amount of counterpoint. Each of the four instruments seems to have some personality of its own. The harmonies are pleasant enough. Some of the melodies are even singable. When it comes down to it, I can't find anything wrong with this piece. Except for one thing. It is not *wonderful*! I think you were much too concerned with not making mistakes when you wrote this piece. It sounds like it."

Several months later I composed my first sonata for violin and piano. Either I had just fallen in love or my gonads had finally kicked in. It was probably a combination of both. In those days I couldn't tell the difference. I'd composed this music so fast and furiously that I could barely get the notes down on paper, let alone worry about anything so trivial as making a few so-called mistakes. Faculty violinist Paul Revitt and pianist-composer Lockrem Johnson sight-read the manuscript for McKay. He was startled. He turned to me and said, "I don't know what holds this piece together! Parts of it make no sense at all to me. It's not the usual sounds from a violin, nor from a piano. But, it's *wonderful*!" He thought for a moment, then added, "Well, you can't rest on your laurels now. What next?"

THE MUSIC DEPARTMENT faculty was remarkably diverse. Violinist Emanuel Zetlin, a Russian, had been concertmaster of the St. Petersburg orchestra. Cellist Eva Heinitz was from Berlin, as was pianist Elsa Geismar. Pianist Berthe

Poncy Jacobson was Swiss. She had studied in Geneva with composer Ernest Bloch, and in Paris with pianist Bernhard Stavenhauser, a student of Liszt. Conductor Stanley Chappell, from England, had been Leonard Bernstein's assistant at Tanglewood. Pianist Edith Woodcock had studied in Paris with Isadore Phillipe. Randolph Hokanson had studied in London with Dame Myra Hess. Wilhelmina Creel Driver had studied piano in Budapest with Bela Bartok and counterpoint with Zoltan Kodaly.

Louise Van Ogle's winter 1947 survey course in the history of Spanish music consisted mostly of our listening to scratchy recordings played on a well-used portable phonograph. She perked us up when we finally made our way to flamenco and some foot-stomping performances by Argentinita, but she really dazzled us when she introduced us to works by Manuel de Falla. I thought it must be the most exciting music ever written. Our homework was dull. It consisted mostly of trying to memorize the birth and death dates of a bewildering number of past and present Spanish composers. But her digressions in class were colorful, unpredictable, and fascinating. She had just received a letter from Sibelius and she read it aloud to us. She had personally met Johannes Brahms and Clara Schumann. Considering that Brahms had died in 1897, you have some idea of Miss Van Ogle's age. She retired the following year.

Edith Woodcock taught piano, musical form, and a course in the Beethoven string quartets. The piano faculty had the greatest esteem for her musicianship. I especially remember her Beethoven class. It was not so much what she said about the quartets. It was the experience of watching the shifting, complex emotions that swept across her face while she listened to them in class with us. She became fully absorbed in the music. Watching her listen to Beethoven was one of the most revealing musical experiences of my student days. When Miss Woodcock retired from teaching she was not one to settle into the comfortable torpor of retirement. She signed up for ballroom dancing lessons and amazed the rest of us with the unexpected flair she had for intricate dance steps. For her ninetieth birthday, she planned to perform Beethoven's *Piano Sonata No. 27, opus 90 in E minor*, at the retirement home where she now lived. Too much fuss was made over this concert-to-be, so she gave a private recital for a few close friends instead.

Music historian Hazel Gertrude Kinscella was a well-known writer of books on music, especially the history of American music. She was a close friend of composer Edward McDowell's widow. She had many stories to tell, mostly about composers and performers she had known. As a pianist, she had once recorded Debussy's "Golliwog's Cakewalk" for one of the major recording companies.

Miss Kinscella was intrigued by my collection of musical autographs. During high school I wrote to dozens of famed musicians for their autographs. In some cases this led to letter exchanges. I received autograph signatures, letters, and sometimes even fragments of original music manuscripts from Stravinsky, Schönberg, Sibelius, Bloch, Shostakovich, Hindemith, de Falla, Bernstein, and countless other contemporary composers, and from song writers Cole Porter, Sigmund Romberg, and Jerome Kern. I wrote to French painter Henri Matisse, to playwright George Bernard Shaw, and even to Albert Einstein. I corresponded with William C. Handy, father of the blues. Coming home from Queen Anne High School each afternoon, I never knew what I would find in the mailbox.

Miss Kinscella encouraged me to save carefully all my letters and notes from composers. "The most casual little note or seemingly incidental remark," she told me, "may in time provide the key to something very interesting. Grocery shopping lists, laundry lists, the most unlikely scraps can often be the most revealing."

Some of the music faculty members had invited me to address them by their first names. Such a familiarity with Hazel Kinscella would have been unthinkable. Year after year I continued to address her as Dr. Kinscella. She finally stopped me in the music department hallway one morning. "Wesley," she said, "you and I have known each other for many years now, long enough that I don't think you need to address me as Dr. Kinscella any longer. From now on, please feel free to address me as Miss Kinscella."

THE CAMPUS MUSIC building was a dilapidated wooden structure. The floor boards creaked. Plaster sometimes dropped off the ceiling as we sat in class. It's a wonder it didn't collapse during the 1947 earthquake! The walls were so thin that music students in adjoining practice rooms could barely hear themselves practicing. Vocalizing sopranos competed with trumpet players. Pianists pounded out the opening chords of Grieg's piano concerto. Somewhere down the hall a violinist was inevitably practicing Mendelsohn's violin concerto. Across campus there were similar practice rooms in the basement of Meany Hall. Student composer Bob Dyke was locally famous for his musical performance called "Meany Hall at Noon." Bob could interchangeably vocalize scales like a soprano, sing like a lovesick tenor, imitate brass instruments, and leap from one piano concerto to the next.

During the late 1940s, there were several young student composers in the music department who were already accomplished composers, including Lockrem Johnson, Gerald Kechley, Paul Tufts, and Gerald Hartley. Lockrem had studied music composition with George McKay and piano with Berthe Poncy Jacobson. He regularly accompanied faculty violinist Emanuel Zetlin and cellist Eva Heinitz when they gave faculty recitals. One evening I heard Lockrem perform his own piano works at the Forestry Department auditorium — in the same hall and on the same piano used by Hungarian composer Bela Bartok during a recital several years earlier. Lockrem's music "spoke" to me in a highly personal way. After the concert I went up to the stage to congratulate him. George McKay introduced us. I mentioned Bartok to them.

"Yes, indeed," said McKay. "You are standing in the very same spot where I introduced Lockrem and my other students to Mr. Bartok a few years ago. I asked him if he had any advice for my student composers. He told them: 'Keep your music simple! Don't try to say everything at once.'"

I began to study piano and composition privately with Lockrem Johnson. I was a terrible student. Lockrem winced as I stumbled through relatively easy pieces by Chopin and Beethoven. He decided that at least I could try being his page turner for concerts. We began to see a great deal of each other and to take trips together on weekends. When he played

chamber music recitals in eastern Washington, I sometimes
went along as his page turner.

Fellow student Audrey Roats was thirtyish. She was di-
vorced and had a small child to support. She offered to help
me cram for finals. We often went out for dinner together.
Some of the other music majors with whom I hung out were
World War II veterans just out of the navy. They had lots of
amorous escapades to brag about, and they enjoyed watching me blush. I also saw a lot of painters Mark Tobey, Morris
Graves, Guy Anderson, and Helmi Juvonen, each of whom
was unmarried.

Voice instructor Alice Cave was blond, attractive, and all
of thirty years old. I was an inexperienced nineteen. Alice
sang two songs of mine with the Seattle Youth Symphony,
with Francis Aranyi conducting. While I was composing
songs for her, I was in and out of her apartment regularly.
Although it was all very innocent, my social life bothered
Hazel Kinscella and some of the other music faculty. Finally,
Miss Kinscella took me aside and told me it would be better
if I spent more time with students my own age. Besides, she
added, it didn't look right for teachers and students to be seen
together so often — and especially taking trips out of town together so often! I asked my mother about this. Her advice was
simple enough: I would have to decide, she said, whether I
was going to have a rich and interesting life, or merely a dull
and conventional existence.

PROFESSOR EILENE RISEGARI'S music harmony assignments were already dull. When she saw some of the
music I was composing, she was upset. "Mr. Wehr," she
said sternly, "you must first learn the rules before you are al-

lowed to break them. Your music is breaking rules before you have even learned what those rules are!" George McKay and Lockrem Johnson were more supportive of what I wrote.

Lockrem went over my compositions carefully. Sometimes he performed them in public. He was a first-rate teacher. He could be wonderfully comic. He could also be bitter, sarcastic, and arrogant. He seemed to think that being cynical was a sign of superiority. He tried very hard to show me how to be a "professional" composer, copying my music scores in the prescribed way, arranging for performances, and sending scores to publishers. I soon became an industrious Lockrem Johnson mini-clone. This pleased Lockrem. But George McKay, watching me carefully from the sidelines, was concerned. One afternoon he stopped me in the music department hallway. "Wesley," he said, "I've been watching you lately. You're becoming very professional in the way you go about everything—like Lockrem. But I must tell you something. There are people in this life who fear they will never be liked nor loved. So they set out to be feared and respected. Lockrem, I am sorry to say, is one of these. These people find out sooner or later that being feared and respected is no substitute for being liked and loved." By now I already knew Lockrem well enough to have seen the bitterness and loneliness just below his surface. McKay was right. Lockrem's ambition seemed driven by some deep personal disappointment.

Lockrem Johnson moved to New York, where he founded his own music publishing company, Dow Music. He wanted to publish music by Northwest composers. He published a piano suite and a song of mine. Neither piece sold very well. A Los Angeles music publisher later republished the piano suite in an anthology of works by composers past and present. As a solo piece it sold poorly. The piano anthology, however, sold quite well, because it contained so many well-known piano pieces by Schubert, Beethoven, Debussy, Bartok, and other masters. I found myself in the odd position of indirectly making some money off of a lot of dead composers. It was the still-living composers such as myself who collected the royalties from the sales of this piano anthology.

THE 1950S WITNESSED the construction of many new buildings on the campus. The old music building was torn down, and a new music building was erected. The walls between the practice rooms in the new music building were better soundproofed than those in the old building. There were more rooms in which the music students could practice. If I were composing a song, I could find sopranos, tenors, and baritones in the third-floor rooms, only a few steps away from my own practice room. If I had just written something for violin and had no idea how it would sound, there were always a few violin students practising down the hall.

BRAZILIAN COMPOSER Heitor Villa-Lobos used the basement band room for several days to rehearse the Seattle Symphony orchestra for a concert of his works. Percussion player Lois Russell performed the parts written for various Brazilian percussion instruments. A few of the student composers, including myself, were allowed to attend the rehearsal, as long as we sat quietly in the corner.

Villa-Lobos did not, we were told, speak English. He would therefore need a translator, a young man who turned out to be something of a musical illiterate. At one point

during the rehearsal, Mr. Villa-Lobos said, "Con sordino!"
The translator stood up and solemnly said to the assembled
orchestra, "The Maestro wishes for you to put on your
mutes now."

Mr. Villa-Lobos was a good conductor, especially of his
own music. He could conduct with a glance. The rehearsal
went along smoothly. Until Mr. Villa-Lobos said, "Pizzicato!"

Up again stood the translator. "Gentlemen, the Maestro
now wishes for you to pluck your strings!"

The orchestra players could barely keep a straight face.
They gaped at each other. "Is this guy for real?," they wondered. At the end of the rehearsal the orchestra members and
those of us in the small audience applauded Mr. Villa-Lobos.
A few of the more perverse music students then turned to the
translator and applauded him.

DURING THE 1930S AND 1940S composer John Cage
was notorious for his avant garde musical innovations. His
music for "prepared piano" required that the piano strings be
modified with different sorts of wires and pieces of wood. The
resultant sounds were bizarre. In 1939 composer Cage was
hired as piano accompanist for Bonnie Bird's dance classes
at the Cornish School in Seattle. He also taught percussion
instruments and conducted his own percussion instrument
orchestra.

Late one morning in the 1960s, Cage and pianist David
Tudor gave a "prepared piano" concert in the music auditorium. After they had performed, they left the concert hall, ne-
glecting to unprepare the prepared piano. Soon after, one of
the piano faculty sat down at the same piano. She was getting
ready to play Bach's *Italian Concerto* in a recital the follow-

ing evening. Bringing her hands dramatically down on the piano keyboard she let out an audible gasp when the piano responded with a cacophonous explosion of tinkles, plinks, thuds, clangs, and clunks. The music professor bolted up from the piano bench and backed away warily from the berserk piano. Shaken, she walked briskly out of the auditorium. Later that afternoon Cage reappeared in the auditorium to restore the piano to its normal condition — unaware of the previous episode.

The following evening, the piano professor walked onto the stage, bowed stiffly to the audience, and moved cautiously toward the piano. She performed that evening with a lack of self-confidence and a distraction that were rare for her. She seemed afraid of the piano now, unconvinced that it might not at any moment turn into a musical monstrosity again and attack her.

I FIRST MET JOHN Cage when I dropped by Mark Tobey's house in the University District one afternoon in 1951. I had just composed a sonata for viola and piano, and I had the manuscript with me. This sonata had even won a prize in a composition for young local composers. The competition had not been formidable. It was a clunky piece, sounding like an inept imitation of German composer Paul Hindemith.

Tobey introduced me to John Cage and suggested I show my music score to him. Mr. Cage glanced quickly through the music, frowning more and more. He handed the score back to me. "It's rather vigorous, isn't it?" was his sole comment. Tobey, observing the strained situation, asked Mr. Cage and me if we would like to have a cup of coffee.

FRENCH COMPOSER-CONDUCTOR Manuel Rosenthal was conductor of the Seattle Symphony during the 1950–53 season. As a young man, Rosenthal had been Maurice Ravel's only private student. Before coming to Seattle, Rosenthal taught briefly at the University of Puget Sound in Tacoma. He and his wife lived on the west side of Queen Anne Hill. For several months I studied privately with him. Every two weeks I took a city bus to his house for my lesson. I had intended to study orchestration with him, but when he realized how unprepared I was, he set me to work doing elementary counterpoint exercises. He was dismayed by my inadequate training in musical counterpoint. "By the age of twelve we know all of this better than you do!" he complained.

Mrs. Rosenthal invariably sat at the dining-room table in the next room while I was having my lesson with her husband. Now and then, Mr. Rosenthal would say something to her in French, just after he had told me again what a poor student I was. Mrs. Rosenthal would glance back at Mr. Rosenthal and shrug her shoulders in a resigned way that began to demoralize me.

I brought new compositions to my lessons. Mr. Rosenthal clearly disliked the first piece I brought him. "Why do you write this 'atonal' kind of thing? I don't care for this kind of music at all. It isn't even well-composed!" he said. Two weeks later I arrived with a new song, a setting of American poet Kenneth Patchen's poem "O, My Darling Troubles Heaven with Her Loveliness." I had even dedicated the song "To Mrs. Manuel Rosenthal," who read the inscription and shot her husband an unfathomable glance. Mr. Rosenthal liked this song somewhat better than the pieces I had brought to my previous lessons. For one thing, it was much more "French."

It lacked any Teutonic overtones. But the lessons cost twenty dollars an hour, a considerable amount of money for then, and I had to discontinue them.

Manuel Rosenthal's stay in Seattle was cut short by a difficult circumstance. His "wife," it turned out, was not his legal wife, who lived in Paris. Being Catholic, Rosenthal and his Parisian wife could not divorce. Somehow this carefully guarded secret was unmasked — by a rival and vindictive Seattle musician, according to the gossip going around town. The newspapers broadcast this "scandalous" news on their front pages. The conductor of the Seattle Symphony was living with a woman "out of wedlock." Several influential women's groups expressed outrage that Seattle's children were attending concerts conducted by "an adulterer." Rosenthal was forced to resign, and Seattle lost a first-rate musician. I ran into faculty cellist Eva Heinitz on campus and broke the news to her. She was unsympathetic. "If I wanted to live with a man," she said, "I'd move to New York. I certainly wouldn't do such a thing here. Manuel should have known better!"

By 1954, I was becoming too much of a permanent fixture around the music department. I had just completed composing my thesis for the Master of Arts degree in music, a set of songs for voice and stringed orchestra. Now it was time for me to appear before the music department's graduate committee to defend my thesis. I arrived for my examination with my thesis printed out on a seemingly endless roll of unfolded pages of music. I unrolled the manuscript like a Chinese scroll along the table of the room where members of the music faculty sat eating lunch.

The examining professors must have been anxious to approve my thesis, grant me a degree, and send me on my way out into the world. Their questions were casual and surprisingly easy to answer. But Professor Demar Irvine perhaps felt I was having too easy a time of it. He asked me a question that was far over my head. Even had I understood his question, I surely would not have answered it adequately. George McKay sat next to me. He sensed my panic. "That's a very good question, Demar," he said. "Wes and I have discussed that interesting matter several times already." McKay glanced quickly at me and I nodded meekly. He proceeded to paraphrase the question and to answer it on my behalf. Professor Irvine sized up the situation and decided not to interrogate me any further. The committee thanked me and continued eating lunch. A few days later I was notified that they had passed me.

IN 1958 FRENCH BARITONE Pierre Bernac was invited by the Cornish School to give a two-week-long master class in the history of the French art song. I had written a good deal of vocal music, so I enrolled in Bernac's master class as a composer. Bernac was considered to be the finest living exponent of French vocal music, one of France's greatest musical treasures. His vocal concerts and recordings with French composer Francois Poulenc were legendary. We awaited his arrival with considerable awe, bracing ourselves for an intimidating two weeks. We encountered instead an amiable and unpretentious man who taught us with great generosity of spirit.

The student singers brought songs by Debussy, Ravel, Fauré, Duparc, Hahn, and Poulenc to sing for Bernac. Some of the students arrived well prepared. A few of them lacked, among other things, any idea of French pronunciation.

Bernac patiently spent part of the class time giving those students who needed it detailed instruction in basic French pronunciation. He never once became condescending or impatient. Indeed, he was so considerate, patient, and self-effacing with his students that it was possible to forget his own consummate artistry. One afternoon, however, when one of the students was singing "C," one of Poulenc's greatest songs, Bernac offered to demonstrate to her another way of singing the opening passage. He nodded to pianist-accompanist Helen Tavernitti to play the opening bars of "C" again. Our drab class room became transformed as Bernac sang. His voice was rapturous and so compelling that the rest of us were transfixed. Nothing else existed. The dingy walls, the folded chairs, the plain wood floor of the classroom disappeared while Bernac's singing became so radiant that everything around him seemed to glow. Then he stopped and turned to the young singer. "You might consider phrasing the opening that way," he said to her.

During the remaining class sessions, Bernac sang passages from other great songs for us, illustrating different ways of interpreting. He was by then perhaps about fifty years old, and many of his greatest performances had been given years before. But even now he introduced his students to supreme levels of artistry as he sang for us.

I asked Mr. Bernac if I might bring some of my own songs to a lesson. Two days later I arrived with a briefcase full of song manuscripts — settings of Shakespeare's "The Wind and the Rain," Matthew Arnold's "Dover Beach," and settings in German of poems by Rilke and Theodor Storm. Mr. Bernac first sang through the setting I had done of a love lyric by Storm.

"Do you speak German?" he asked me.

"No, I don't."

"This setting is rather good. If you don't speak German, how did you manage to set the words to music as well as you did?"

"Nora Haimberger, a pianist friend from Germany, taught me to recite this poem in German. Then I set it to music."

Mr. Bernac sang through the other songs I had brought. I would not have imagined that anything I composed could ever sound so convincing as these songs of mine did when Mr. Bernac sang them.

"I have some advice for you," Mr. Bernac concluded. "Even though your settings in German are actually quite good, German is not your native language. When you compose music for songs in English, I can feel that you are in your own language. I would suggest you concentrate for now on setting the English language to music. I've noticed that American singers seem to have an inclination to sing in different languages too early in their training. There is time later for that. It is difficult enough to master the singing of songs in one's own language, and especially so when one's native country is not multilingual."

By the end of the two weeks of master classes we, his students, had become so fond of this kind man and great musician that it was very difficult to bid him goodbye.

Ernest Bloch
at Agate Beach

SWISS-AMERICAN MUSICIAN Ernest Bloch was a composer of the most exacting integrity, a towering and singular figure in twentieth century music. From 1940 until his death in 1959 he lived with his wife at Agate Beach, Oregon, in a large house that overlooked the Pacific Ocean and the Yaquina Bay lighthouse. His neighbors told me they were vaguely aware he composed music, but mostly they knew him as an amiable and somewhat solitary man who frequently strolled the beaches, collecting agates, stopping now and then to chat with some of the people who lived there.

Lockrem Johnson had introduced me to many of Bloch's works, to the *Concerto Grosso No. I*, the *Quintet for Piano and Strings*, and the *Second String Quartet*. Pianist Berthe Poncy Jacobson had studied with Bloch in Geneva. His music evoked for me images of the Oregon Coast — its winter storms and tumultuous ocean surf, and the vast expanses of the coastlines and distant horizon. I eventually dedicated a work to him, my "Canticle for piano and stringed orchestra."

Several of my fellow music students had met Ernest Bloch personally. Student composer-pianist Bob Dyke had spent an afternoon and evening with Bloch at Agate Beach. Student composer Hubbard Miller, as the story goes, had once been beachcombing at Agate Beach. He paused on the beach to trace some musical staves in the sand, and then added the opening notes of Beethoven's *Fifth Symphony*. Hub had, however, made a slight mistake. Instead of using eighth notes for the famous "da, da, da, *dum!*," Hub had written a triplet. He had the right notes, but the wrong rhythm — an easy enough mistake for a young lad to make. Hub looked up to find an elderly man standing beside him, studying the musical misnotation. The mysterious man erased the mistake with one foot, bent down, and wrote the correct rhythmic notation in the sand. With that, he smiled at Hub and continued walking down the beach. Only later did Hub learn that he had just had a "music lesson" from Ernest Bloch.

DURING THE CHRISTMAS HOLIDAY of 1954, piano student Bob Kuykendall and I took a Greyhound bus to the Oregon coast to go rockhounding. We also hoped to encounter Ernest Bloch, whom we'd never met. We got off at Newport and took a room in an old hotel on Yaquina Bay. After dinner we made plans. The next morning, Bob and I beachcombed from Nye Beach to Agate Beach. The winter storms had uncovered the beach sands, leaving moonstone, carnelian, and cloud agates glistening in the beach gravels. When we arrived at the small settlement at Agate Beach, we went to a coffee

Ernest Bloch with his cat, Gris-Gris, at Agate Beach, Oregon, 1958
(Photograph by Lucienne Bloch Dimitroff, courtesy of the estate)

shop to try to figure out what to do next. Ernest Bloch's house was just across the road. Bob's approach was so simple. "Let's just go over and knock on Mr. Bloch's door and see what happens!"

When we arrived at their house, Mrs. Bloch answered the door. She invited us in, saying, "Mr. Bloch is just finishing his lunch. If you'll please wait for him in the living room, he'll join you in a few minutes."

Shortly after that, Ernest Bloch entered the room.

"I'm a very busy man, you realize — so I can't visit with you for very long today. Are you music students?" he asked.

"Yes, I said. "Bob studies piano at the University of Washington, and I study music composition there. Berthe Poncy Jacobson asked that we convey her warm regards to you."

Bloch looked puzzled. "Berthe Poncy Jacobson?" He paused, trying to place the name. Suddenly he broke into a smile. "Berthe *Poncy*! Oh, she was my best student in Geneva. And she was so beautiful. Who could forget her? How *is* she? I'm so happy to hear her name again after all these years. Such a fine musician — a true artist. You're very fortunate she's in Seattle and teaching music there. Please tell her that I send my very best regards."

Bob Kuykendall and I apologized for intruding upon his time, but Mr. Bloch invited us to visit with him for a while. The mere mention of Berthe Poncy Jacobson's name had brought back such happy memories that he wanted to hear more about her. After that we asked him about his composing. Was he working on a particular piece of music?

"I'm composing an orchestral work now [*Symphony in E flat major*, 1954–55]," he answered. "The first three movements went rather quickly, but the last movement has been very difficult to write. It's only some four minutes of music, but a point has come when there are several directions which the music can now take. There are various solutions. I realize that there is only one *right* one. Buried somewhere in the earlier movements is the source which I have to find again. It means tracing the music backwards, following the work back to its very roots. It's a mistake to *force* the act of composition, you know. The growth and flow of a work should be natural.

"So I worked in the garden this morning. I walked along the beach, looking for agates — things to refresh my mind. The right and *only* solution will come with patience and of its own accord. It will not be a mechanical answer to the musical problem, but a natural growth and development of the musical ideas. You see, a piece of music is like a plant. It grows from a seed and everything in it is contained in that initial seed. The composer has to let that musical seed grow and flourish according to its nature. Like a plant, he must prune it here and there. But he shouldn't force its growth with artificial fertilizers and merely clever musical solutions to the difficulties which arise in composing it." He smiled at us, pausing for a moment before he continued.

"Living here by the sea, and working in my garden, I'm reminded constantly of how important it is that I strive for the natural and genuine in my music. I'm like a plant myself — I have to grow according to my deepest nature. If I hadn't become a composer, I probably would have been a botanist. Often, when I'm composing, I'll stop and go out into my garden to tend the plants. Then I'm with living things again. That clarifies what I try to do with my music!"

MR. BLOCH ASKED BOB which composers and which of their piano works he was studying. He asked me about my technical training as a composer. Was I, he wanted to know, receiving a solid background in musical counterpoint and traditional musical forms?

"I'm still a music student myself, even at my advanced age [74 years old]," he said. "I'm studying Beethoven's *Eroica Symphony* again. What a great masterpiece it is—the music of a giant! I'll come to a certain moment in that symphony where Beethoven has to decide what he is going to do next. I'll write down all the possible solutions I can think of— where the symphony can go next. After I've done that, I'll look at the score again to see what Beethoven did. And his solution is always the right one, the inspired one.

"I always study Bach's *Well-Tempered Clavier*. People may call me 'old hat,' but there is so very much that the truly great masters like Beethoven and Bach have yet to teach me. I'll be their student as long as I live. When a student comes to work with me, we study music together. If it's the music of Debussy, I want my student to know and feel something about the time in which Debussy lived and composed. I want him to read the great writers of that period, know how people dressed, know something about their conventions. He should understand the atmosphere and sensibilities of Debussy's Paris."

LOCKREM JOHNSON had introduced me to Ernest Bloch's string quartets. I told Mr. Bloch that there were passages in his string quartets that evoked for me the ocean and infinite distances, much like the view out his window across the room. Was he still composing chamber music, I asked him? Yes, he answered.

"When I've finished a new string quartet, the Griller Quartet comes here to Agate Beach to play through it, and we work together on it. There's a rather nice restaurant across the road from this house. Perhaps you noticed it. The food there can be quite good. After our work session, sometimes I'll go there with the quartet for dinner. We go on discussing how to improve the new work, or we may talk about mutual friends. They are very fine musicians. I like to visit with them, and it's a real pleasure to work with them."

BOB KUYKENDALL ASKED Mr. Bloch if he had any private students working with him. No, Mr. Bloch answered. He was no longer teaching. He did, however, talk about his having been a teacher.

"When Herbert Elwell first came to study with me," he said, "there was something very nice about his counterpoint exercises. They had that quality which we call bittersweet — and life itself, when you think about it, is often bittersweet. A strange mixture of happiness and discontent. Then Elwell went away for a while to study and listen to what other composers were writing. When he came back to see me, he showed me what he had composed. But it wasn't his own simple, lovely music anymore. It had some Stravinsky in it, and some Bloch. It sounded like many people. I was very disappointed. I told him that he would have to find his way back to what was genuinely his own, composed from his heart. He'd neglected everything which made his music genuine, and he'd replaced it with all the fashionable 'isms' of that time.

"I'm quite an old man now. I've lived through every 'ism' since Cesar Franck's chromaticism. I've completely lost track of how many of them have come and gone since that one.

Every time there was a new ism, people would say, 'Oh, this is *it*!' And that would be the thing we were all supposed to chase after. But then that ism would fade away and there would be still another one, and then still another one. After I had seen about twenty or so of these isms come and go, one day I said to myself, 'Well, Ernest Bloch, what are you going to do about all of these isms? What do they really have to do with *you*?' Then it became very clear to me that there was really only one thing I could do. I had to take my own pulse, listen to my own heart, and go on in my own way. After that I wasn't very concerned with all those isms any more."

MR. BLOCH ASKED Bob Kuykendall and me about what we did when we weren't practicing the piano and studying music. Did we, he asked, have any hobbies? What did we do for recreation? Describing his own student days, he told us: "In Switzerland, when we were students, we used to work very hard during the week, and during the weekends we would go hiking in our beautiful mountains, or we'd go skiing. That was our refreshment. We knew how to work and we knew how to renew ourselves. But you American students often have some notion that if you work *seven* days a week, you'll accomplish more. What happens then is that you lose your concentration. You work like drones, and the results are joyless and mechanical."

MR. BLOCH WONDERED HOW WE HAD come to knock on his door that afternoon. "When you first arrived today, you told me that you were staying in Newport. How did you come up to Newport? Did you drive up?" he asked.

"No," I answered. "We walked from Newport along the

beach. We wanted to look for agates, and we found some really beautiful ones. We came here from Seattle hoping we might be able to meet you, even for a minute or two. Finally we ended up in the cafe across the road. We sat there for a long time, drinking coffee, and trying to decide if we really should intrude upon you this way."

Bob and I reached into our jacket pockets and pulled out several dozen beach agates which we had found that morning. Mr. Bloch was delighted.

"Agates! You like agates too? You should have mentioned that sooner. I not only collect them on the beach, I polish them myself. Did you notice the two-storey garage beside the path when you came to my house? In one room I have a piano and I compose there. In a room next to it, I have my agate-polishing equipment. Come with me. I'll show you some of my collection."

As we started toward the hallway, we passed a large wooden Christ figure above a bookcase. Mr. Bloch, seeing that I was looking at it, stopped. "Knowing that I'm Jewish, perhaps you're surprised to see this figure of Christ in my home," he said. "But it is *art*, and such a moving sculpture. It conveys so well not only the suffering of Christ but all human suffering as well. There are things that go beyond religious differences, and this work of art is one of them."

We left the living room and entered a long narrow hallway. On the left I glimpsed a small, simply furnished bedroom. Mr. Bloch opened a door on the right, and we entered a small room. There were shelves stacked with cigar boxes. Looking for his agates, he opened one cigar box. It was filled with ornate documents and certificates. He flicked through them with some impatience.

"Oh, these things. These are the scraps of paper they give to a composer when they decide to make him an official museum piece. They don't really mean very much to me. My agates are much more interesting. Can you guess how people got rid of me as a composer? I used to compose music which upset them so much. They said it was too dissonant and modern. It hurt their ears to listen to it. One day they finally had enough of being upset by what I composed, so they decided to call me a 'grand old master.' What that really amounted to was that they were putting me on the shelf. They wouldn't have to think about me anymore or listen to my music anymore. They could just say, 'Ernest Bloch is an old master,' and go back to listening to the insipid music which didn't offend their poor little ears. You see, giving fancy honors and titles to an artist is one sure way of dismissing him — honoring his reputation and ignoring his actual work."

He picked up a dark grey stone from the table. On its surface was a small, scarablike fossil trilobite. "Do you know what this is? It's a trilobite, and it's very ancient. Millions and millions of years old," he said.

He opened another cigar box. "Oh, here are my agates. Why don't you take some of them for yourselves — take more than that. I have many of them. I'll give you a little box to put them in. And — oh, yes — I want you especially to give one to Berthe Poncy . . . Jacobson. Please tell her that it's a little gift from Ernest Bloch, and that he remembers her very well. Now please be sure to do that for me!"

WE RETURNED TO THE LIVING ROOM and sat down again. Mr. Bloch was quiet for a few moments and then he looked up at us. Speaking very slowly and softly, he said, "You know, life is a very strange thing. Sometimes it is filled with so many disappointments. Things that one wants and can't have. Things that go wrong, and there just doesn't seem to be anything that you can do about it. Sometimes there are so many disappointments that gradually one just starts to get used to them. You start to live with them in some kind of resignation. But then—sometimes—a remarkable thing happens. Just as you've grown resigned to being disappointed, and have almost learned how to live with it, life will spring a *joy* on you. Something you never expected. A wonderful surprise. What I am trying to tell you is that life is so unpredictable and so strange that you can't even count on your unhappiness and disappointments."

It was growing late in the afternoon. The winter sunlight that had been streaming into the room was darkening. We had stayed for quite a while, and it was time to leave. Mr. Bloch saw us to the door, and we stepped out into the garden with him. He stood for a moment, looking at us, and then extended his hand.

"I won't say goodbye. Because perhaps we'll meet again. Maybe on the beach. You never know. The world is a very strange place," he said, as he walked back into his house, pausing to wave at us from the front door.

AFTER THE VISIT was over, Bob and I were euphoric. We bought two six-packs of beer in a tavern along the coastal highway from Bloch's house. We walked up the steep road to the Yaquina lighthouse and edged our way out onto a precipitous basalt ledge to watch the sun go down. It began to grow dark. The gusts of wind bent the tree boughs. The lights at Newport five miles down the beach were gradually coming on. We made our way to the moonlit beach and stumbled drunkenly in the surf, splashing each other with sea water. Drenched and oblivious, we walked back to town along the beach, returned to our hotel room at Yaquina Bay, and collapsed on our hotel beds. We blinked at each other. Had we really just spent the day with Ernest Bloch? Had we really seen the view of the windswept trees outside his living room window, the Pacific ocean surf, and the Yaquina lighthouse? The stillness and beauty of the Oregon Coast were unforgettable.

THE NEXT DAY BOB and I caught a Greyhound bus for Seattle. Mr. Bloch had given us a small box filled with beach agates and asked us to make a point of giving one of these agates to Mrs. Jacobson. Bob and I knocked on her door the following day and presented a banded carnelian agate to her. Mr. Bloch had collected it on the beach below his house and had hand-polished it on his lapidary equipment. Mrs. Jacobson was skeptical at first. "Did Mr. Bloch really remember me? Did he really say those nice things about me?" she asked. It obviously meant a great deal to her that Bloch remembered her so warmly. From that day on, she always carried Bloch's hand-polished agate in her purse. Sometimes Mrs. Jacobson would open her purse and show the agate to me again. "See, I always keep this agate with me now!"

Berthe Poncy
Jacobson

W HEN I BEGAN MY STUDIES in the music department during January 1947, I immediately started to
hear about Berthe Poncy Jacobson. She was head of piano
studies. She was also, I was told, one of painter Mark Tobey's
closest friends. Many years earlier, she had studied with
Ernest Bloch in Geneva, and she was a graduate of the great
Schola Cantorum in Paris, where she had studied with composer Vincent d'Indy and pianist Blanche Selva. She had also
studied with Bernhard Stavenhauser, a student of Franz Liszt.
Before joining the music faculty at the University of Washington, Mrs. Jacobson was on the piano faculty at the Cornish
School in Seattle.

Mrs. Jacobson was held in an esteem by the music faculty and students at the University of Washington that approached reverence. I was told that she could have a biting

and impatient tongue, that she had an unpredictable sense of humor, and that her worldly sophistication was of an order that set her apart. I also learned that she seldom performed in public, but when she did, it was a rare musical experience.

I wanted to meet her. My introduction must have made a lasting impression on her because many years later she said: "I haven't forgotten the first time we met. I heard a knock on my studio door. When I opened the door, I saw a very shy young boy. 'Henry Matisse just sent me his autograph. Would you like to see it?' he asked me. —With an opening line like that, you had me!"

ONCE A WEEK Mark Tobey went to Mrs. Jacobson's house in Laurelhurst for dinner and a private piano lesson. He was somewhat in awe of her, and she was deeply fond of him. Tobey knew many people in Seattle. He was often invited out minus his companion Pehr Hallsten, who could be socially unpredictable, the proverbial bull in the china closet. Tobey's weekly evenings with Mrs. Jacobson were especially important to him. Mrs. Jacobson, for that matter, considered her friendship with Tobey to be of such a personal nature that, so far as I can determine, several weeks before she died she destroyed not only her private diaries but also her letters from Tobey.

Mrs. Jacobson was a very private person. She complained sharply about Americans' total disregard for an individual's privacy. Her own integrity — both musically and personally — were beyond reproach. By the same token she had little use for people who themselves lacked character. "I don't go looking for trouble. I have enough of it already. If I don't like someone, I avoid him," she explained.

Berthe Poncy Dow (Jacobson) as a faculty member at the
Cornish School of the Arts, Seattle, 1927 (Photograph from the
collection of Gordon Grant)

She invited painter Gary Lundell and me to her house to dye Easter eggs. Pianist Randolph Hokanson and his wife, composer Dorothy Cadzow Hokanson, would also be there. They had just bought two of Gary's landscape paintings. Mrs. Jacobson owned one of Gary's paintings too. She found it "very musical!" She answered the door and invited Gary and me in, saying that she had just finished listening to some contemporary music on the radio. "I listened to some works by Berio and Stockhausen. I couldn't make anything at all out of them. But then I'm Swiss and I'm set in my ways. I'm sure these works do have their own beauty. But I didn't experience it today.

"Many years ago, when I was studying with Bloch in Geneva," she continued, "he came back from hearing the premier of *Pelleas and Melisande* in Paris. He described for us his experience of hearing *Pelleas* for the first time: 'There I sat listening to Debussy's music. Even though it had many beautiful sounds, it seemed so amorphous to me. But I didn't judge this music quickly. I continued to listen to it very patiently. Then I heard a melody. And then another melody. Before I knew it, *Pelleas* was filled with the most beautiful melodies! I started to understand this music. It had taken patience on my part. What I am trying to tell you now is that the truly new music doesn't reveal its beauty immediately. You must grow to appreciate it. And that takes time!'"

Mrs. Jacobson fell silent. She seemed lost in some private reflection. "That was an important lesson for me, hearing Mr. Bloch tell us that. He made me realize the importance of patience when we encounter something new and different in our lives," she finally said.

Cellist Eva Heinitz, Berthe Poncy Jacobson, and clarinettist Ronald Phillips in rehearsal at the University of Washington, early 1950s (Photograph by James Sneddon, courtesy of University of Washington Libraries)

WHEN I COMPLETED MY GRADUATE STUDIES in music composition under composer John Verrall, Mrs. Jacobson took me out for lunch in the student cafeteria. We finished eating and lit up cigarettes. "You have your master's degree now. Congratulations," she said. She paused, inhaled her cigarette and elegantly exhaled. "Now that you have it, I suppose you've been thinking that you should *do* something with your degree. Has it occurred to you *not* to do anything with your degree? Mark doesn't have a degree. Would you like to be like him? John Verrall has a degree, and he did something with it. Which of them would you prefer to be like — Mark Tobey or John Verrall?" Many years later, I reminded Mrs. Jacobson of what she had said. She was alarmed. "Did I *really* say that to you? I certainly was outspoken!"

MRS. JACOBSON DISLIKED SHOW-OFFS. She wanted little to do with aggressive people. "Aggressive people may get their own way for a while, but only for a while," she said. She was, however, to discover something surprising about herself. Her piano student Billy Chung was becoming well known as a pianist. A local television station wanted to film him playing the piano. Mrs. Jacobson consented to their using her living room and piano for the occasion. "I made it very clear," she told me, "that I would not be a part of it. I would sit across the room while they televised Billy. He and I started talking about piano playing as he was being filmed. I went over to the piano to show him how to play a certain passage. Before I knew it, both Billy and I were being filmed. I discovered that I didn't mind it at all. In fact, I realized something about myself — that I have a bit of the 'ham' in me! It would appear that I'm only human too."

THE LIVING ROOM in Mrs. Jacobson's Laurelhurst house was one of the loveliest rooms I have ever visited. I could never figure out exactly what it was that made that room so magically different. Was it the quality of the diffused light in the room, or the view of the garden outside the window? There were other houses with similar attractions. Was it the furnishings—so simple and in such inconspicuously fine taste? Was it Mark Tobey's *Gothic* hung above the mantle? ("Mark gave that painting to me in exchange for piano lessons," Mrs. Jacobson explained.) Other beautiful Tobeys hung on the walls. On the wall next to the grand piano, I noticed a wonderful little oil landscape, a rustic scene. It was very small, but its radiance made it seem larger than it was.

"I love that painting! Who painted it, anyway?" I asked.

Mrs. Jacobson was pleased I had noticed the picture. "My father painted that," she answered.

All of these things must have had something to do with the spell of that living room. But most of all, one felt how intimately the room reflected Mrs. Jacobson herself.

MRS. JACOBSON WAS PONDERING SOMETHING. She grew quiet, looking at me. "I've just been thinking," she said, "that you have known some remarkable people during the years I have known you. You've known Mark, of course. You've also known Ernest Bloch. And you've known Pierre Bernac. Two great musicians. And other remarkable people. I was just wondering to myself how you came to know them?"

I heard myself saying, "Opportunities arose . . ."

"That's it! That's it exactly!," Mrs. Jacobson exclaimed, cutting me off in midsentence. "Opportunities arose, and you were quick to recognize them as such. You weren't aggressive about it. I don't like aggressive people! You weren't aggressive in meeting these people. Opportunities arose, as you say, and you took it from there."

WE TALKED ABOUT MUSIC that afternoon. Mrs. Jacobson was trying to explain something to me about playing the piano—about the distinction she made between "technique" (which she called the "expressiveness" of music) and the merely "mechanical" aspects of playing the piano. "Technique," she said, "is not mechanical. It's the expressiveness itself." She could not convey to me what she wanted to say. She went to the piano and sat before the keys for a moment. She raised her hands and looked at them. Arthritis had gnarled them. "Look at these hands," she said. "I just can't do all the things with them that I have always been able to do before. Of course, I can't!" With this she carefully placed her right hand on the piano keys and ever so slowly began to play a very simple phrase from Bach. I would never have believed that so much expressiveness and perfection could have been possible with those arthritic hands. When she had finished, she lifted her hands from the piano and turned to me. "You see, I work with what I have. These hands of mine can still express something—if I go about it very carefully. You see, I am not the kind of person who feels sorry for himself and laments his fate. Not at all! Whatever I am, I'm realistic!"

MRS. JACOBSON WAS NOT ONE to complain about whatever difficulties she was experiencing as she grew older and gradually infirm. She either avoided the subject or made light of it. "Recently I wrote to an old friend of mine," she told me. "I was going through a rather low time, my spirits were down. But I didn't want to burden my friend with all my problems. She had enough of her own problems without having to listen to mine. So I wrote a very pleasant letter to her. I only talked about nice things. I left out all the things that were privately getting me down. To show you how well my friend knew me, she wrote me back a nice letter. But at the end of it she wrote: 'I enjoyed your letter very much, dear Berthe. But next time please leave in the bass notes!'"

MRS. JACOBSON TURNED EIGHTY. "When I awake each morning I feel so fortunate. It is one more day I can enjoy and appreciate even more than before — because it seems like a gift at this point in my life." Shortly after that, following a very brief illness, Mrs. Jacobson died. The next morning in Basel, his friend Mark Ritter told me, Mark Tobey came down the stairs from his bedroom. He was pale and shaken. "Someone very dear to me has just died," he announced to Mark Ritter. Hours later Tobey received a cablegram from Seattle notifying him of Mrs. Jacobson's death. Pehr had died ten years earlier, and now Mrs. Jacobson. Tobey himself would die in Basel a few years later.

PETER HALLOCK, CHOIR MASTER at Saint Mark's Cathedral on Capitol Hill, organized a memorial concert for Mrs. Jacobson. Eva Heinitz performed a sarabande from one of Bach's cello suites. The ancient music sung by the choir was deeply moving. I phoned Mrs. Jacobson's close friend, Miriam Terry, several days later. We talked at length about Mrs. Jacobson and our mutual friendship with her.

"Mrs. Jacobson guarded her privacy carefully," I said.

"Yes, and now she is in the most private place there is," responded Miriam.

SHORTLY BEFORE SHE DIED, Berthe Poncy Jacobson attended the unveiling of Mark Tobey's mural at the Opera House at the Seattle Center. She stood alone on the stair landing, carefully studying the mural. As I came down the stairs and paused beside her, she turned to me and said: "You know, growing old is not all that bad after all. There are some things to be said for it. For instance, there comes a time in one's life when you no longer have to be anything. Then you can start to be something for the first time. And there comes a time when you no longer need other people anymore. Then, for the first time you are free to truly love them." With that, Mrs. Jacobson looked once more about the crowded room, continued walking down the Opera House stairs, and disappeared into the summer evening twilight.

Margaret Hamilton:
The Wicked Witch of the West

ACTOR MARGARET HAMILTON IS BEST KNOWN for her portrayal of the Wicked Witch of the West in the original *Wizard of Oz* film that starred Judy Garland, Bert Lahr, Ray Bolger, Jack Haley, and Billie Burke. She also appeared with Mae West and W. C. Fields in *My Little Chickadee*, and with Katharine Hepburn and Spencer Tracy in *State of the Union*. Pop artist Andy Warhol's "Living Icons" portfolio of lithographs includes an acid-green portrait of Miss Hamilton as the Wicked Witch.

During the Christmas holidays of 1968, actor Marjorie Nelson and her husband, architect Victor Steinbrueck, invited me to a holiday party at their house. I arrived there to find that almost everyone else at the party was either an actor or somehow connected with the theater. My attempts to converse with people around the buffet table were inept and uncomfortable. I stacked my plate with Christmas cookies, several sandwiches, took a cup of coffee with me, and retreated to a nearby sofa. At least I could sit, listen, and observe.

A woman, perhaps in her sixties, arrived. Immediately she was surrounded by several talkative young men. She listened attentively to them, barely saying anything, nodding in tacit agreement now and then. One of the young men gallantly lit a cigarette for her. I didn't have a clue as to who she was, but she had an unobtrusive presence about her. In comparison to this unassuming guest, some of the other party guests seemed too jovially self-conscious and a bit theatrical. A few minutes later, this mysterious guest walked across the room and sat beside me on the sofa.

"I assume you're in the theater too. Everyone else at this party seems to be," she said.

"Oh, no. I don't know anything about acting and the theater. I'm a painter," I replied.

"That's wonderful!" she responded. "I would like to have been a painter myself, but I had no talent for it! I was a schoolteacher before I took up acting. Do tell me about yourself. What sort of paintings do you paint?"

Marjorie came across the room to join us. "I see you've already met Margaret Hamilton," she said. Then it dawned on me. This inconspicuous, cordial, and charming woman was the original "Wicked Witch of the West!" The same woman who had scared the hell out of me as a child as I sat spellbound watching *The Wizard of Oz*.

MARGARET HAMILTON WAS IN SEATTLE to perform at the Seattle Repertory Theater as Mrs. Malaprop in

Margaret Hamilton in Seattle, 1973
(Photograph courtesy of the Seattle Times)

Richard Sheridan's *The Rivals*. She had rented a small apartment on the south side of Queen Anne Hill, near the Seattle Center and the Repertory Theater. "I'm performing in a play here. The dress rehearsal is tomorrow, in case you would like to attend. I could leave a ticket for you at the box office," she said. The next day, I watched the rehearsal and walked with her back to her apartment. We exchanged phone numbers. That evening she phoned me, "This is Maggie Hamilton. Please do call me Maggie. Everyone else does. I need some help from you. I'm just not getting a single laugh in the second act. I know that there's at least one line that is funny. People should be laughing at it."

"Which line is it?" I asked.

"When I face the two young people on stage and say, 'Oh, if your father were only alive, this would kill him!' That's a good line, but the audience doesn't laugh. Do you have any suggestions?"

Margaret had tended to run the words together — "this-wouldkillhim." The sense of the line was lost in blurred enunciation. The line was funny enough, but it needed a different articulation, I suspected.

"Try this," I suggested. "Try saying it this way: 'This . . . would . . . k-i-l-l-l-l him!' Let that word *kill* plunge down the musical scale like a slide trombone. Change your vocal color on that word."

All I was doing was trying to remember some things poet Theodore Roethke had taught us about word accentuation and tonal color.

Margaret weighed the suggestion. "I'll think about it tonight. I may even try it out tomorrow," she said.

At the performance the next day she did a great imitation of a slide trombone. The audience laughed loudly. I met her backstage after the performance and walked with her back to her apartment. "Thanks to you, I finally got my laugh in Act Two!" she said.

I was so pleased with myself, silently patting myself on my head. Until, that is, Margaret sized up the situation with a sidelong glance. "Forget it, dear. There's a lot more to being a director than coming up with one good bit of advice!" she said. That was the first time Margaret read my mind. There would be many other times in the coming years when she seemed to be jumps ahead of me.

When I visited New York during 1969 and 1972, Margaret invited me to use her Gramercy Park apartment. She presented me with an apartment key, telling me, "Sometimes people in New York can be somewhat snobbish. Please feel free to give my Gramercy Park address as your New York address. It's a good address to have here."

Margaret was appearing as Aunt Eller in the revival of *Oklahoma!* at Lincoln Center when I stayed with her during 1969. After the overture, the curtains parted. She sat alone in the center of the stage as the orchestra played "Oh, What a Beautiful Morning!" She was seated behind a wooden butter churn, in front of the farmhouse. She unfortunately had come down with a cold which left her hoarse. Except for the performances, her physician had instructed her not to use her voice at all.

Between performances Margaret and I worked out a communication method. When her apartment phone rang, I would answer it and repeat the incoming message aloud to her. She in turn wrote her response on a scrap of paper, which I would read back to the caller on the phone. For several days all of my other exchanges with Margaret consisted of her quickly scrawled notes. This means of communication was time-consuming, but I eventually amassed a large collection of handwritten messages. I later donated these notes and all my letters from her to the University of Washington Library's Manuscripts, Special Collections, University Archives Division.

ON MARCH 6, 1973, I was in New York for the opening of an exhibition of my landscape paintings at the Shepherd Galleries. That evening was the occasion for an improbable meeting of two remarkable women, each of whom lived in a world entirely apart from that of the other – Margaret Hamilton and philosopher Susanne K. Langer. I had invited them to the preview but had not had the opportunity to introduce them to each other. Not having any idea who the other was, they met accidentally in front of a group of my paintings. A friend of mine, pianist Robert Mony, was in earshot when Margaret exclaimed to the stranger beside her, "I just *love* Wes's paintings. I'd like to own *all* of them!"

Susanne, with her customary restraint, answered, "I do think several of these paintings are quite good."

Margaret was dumbfounded by this tepid response. She walked quickly across the room to our mutual friend, pianist Gordon Grant, and asked him indignantly, "Gordie, who's that wet blanket over there, anyway?"

The next day I tried to explain to Susanne that Margaret Hamilton was the Wicked Witch of the West in the original *Wizard of Oz* film. Susanne responded curtly, "I never saw that film! I never had time for that sort of stuff. I was much too busy doing my philosophical work!"

AFTER THE PREVIEW the previous evening, Margaret had taken me out for a celebration dinner. She insisted I order some of the most luxurious items on the menu—the Maine lobster, a fine French wine, the chocolate soufflé! "Live it up, dear. Tonight you opened in New York! You may likely have other shows here in years to come. But it will never be the same. And I'm so happy that I can celebrate this special evening with you!"

The waitress came up to our table. Margaret exclaimed to her, "Why, you look like Simone Signoret!" The waitress, who was actually quite pretty but somewhat plump, was startled. "I think I look like Toti Fields!"

"Oh, no," exclaimed Margaret emphatically, "I have met both women, and I can assure you that you look much more like Simone Signoret than like Toti Fields!" The waitress was flustered, but visibly pleased. She had no idea who Margaret was, and Margaret was not about to tell her.

MARGARET'S GRAMERCY PARK APARTMENT became my New York home away from home. There was a Steinway grand piano in the living room. In the evenings I would play a few pieces for her—a few, because that's all I could remember. A small drum and a padded stick sat on top of the piano. They appeared to be very old. When Margaret saw me looking at them, she tapped the drum ever so gently. "This is a drum for waking Buddha. I was given it when I was in India visiting my family," she explained. The sound of this drum was unlike any musical sound I had ever heard before or since — soft, compelling, haunting. If there had indeed been a drum to wake Buddha, I could believe it was a drum such as this.

During the evenings Margaret worked in her study next to the kitchen, rehearsing for her next TV commercial — as Aunt Cora for Maxwell House coffee. I could hear her trying out lines, rewriting them, speaking them aloud again. She worked very hard to speak those lines to her own satisfaction. Her arch rival was Mrs. Olson, who appeared in a different TV commercial. In a cheery, dubiously Swedish accent, Mrs. Olson extolled the rich flavor of Folger's coffee. I checked Margaret's kitchen cabinets to see which kind of coffee she was actually using. It turned out to be neither. She had freeze-dried Yuban coffee on her shelf!

Although she had appeared in numerous films besides *The Wizard of Oz*, Margaret never received ongoing royalties or income from these movies. Oddly enough, after her long career in the theater and movies, it was her Maxwell House coffee commercials that earned so many royalties that she could set up a trust fund for her grandchildren.

Another windfall for Margaret took place a year or so later, when Pop artist Andy Warhol produced a series of original lithographs depicting famous American "icons." He included Margaret as the Wicked Witch of the West. She was delighted with the results. Warhol depicted her in brilliantly acid-green colors, shrieking and cackling malevolently. When the portfolio was completed, Warhol presented Margaret with about ten original signed lithographs. She realized how valuable they already were. "Thanks to Andy, now I have something to give my grandchildren. These prints will help pay for their college educations," she told me.

MY ART EXHIBITION preview was already a thing of the past. I had been to Old Lyme, Connecticut, and Kingston, New York, with Susanne Langer for some beachcombing and fossil hunting. I returned to New York and stayed with Margaret. We both settled into the pleasant rhythms of a more normal life. I spent the afternoons visiting art and natural history museums, the zoo, and getting together with old friends from Seattle who now lived in New York. Several New York gallery dealers had seen my show at the Shepherd Galleries and sent messages that they would like to talk with me privately. I didn't answer any of these messages. I liked my dealers at the Shepherd Galleries very much and I had no intention of scouting out another gallery. Several friends told me I was a fool, that I was throwing away my "big chance." All they could talk about usually was their "career moves." I vaguely understood what they were getting at, but I was in New York for different reasons from theirs.

One morning over coffee in Margaret's kitchen, while she was reading the *New York Times* and I was writing postcards to Seattle, Margaret put her newspaper down and looked at me very seriously. "You're in New York, dear," she said, "You've just opened an art exhibition, it's all going very well for you. People here like your paintings, and they like you. But I do have some advice for you. And that is, don't ever let anyone take the wind out of your sails. Especially the people who tell you that they love you!" With that, she went back to reading the *New York Times*.

SEVERAL DAYS LATER an attractive, somewhat shy young girl and her boyfriend came to Margaret's apartment. The young lady sat on a floor cushion. Looking reverently up at

Margaret, she announced: "Miss Hamilton, I want to be an actor. Do you have any advice for me?"

Without any hesitation, Margaret answered, "Yes, take up typing!" The aspiring young actor blinked. Margaret continued, "You see, dear, if you know how to type you can be paying the rent between jobs by typing professionally. You'll probably need that extra income. Sometimes jobs are few and far between in the theater. As for how you become an actor, all I can suggest is that you study people, everyone, very carefully. Watch how people walk, how they move. Listen to how they talk. All of that observing comes in very handy at one time or another."

DURING THE EARLY 1970S, Margaret appeared as Madame Arcadi in the Seattle Repertory Theater's production of Noel Coward's *Blithe Spirit*. Margaret also visited Seattle for brief vacations and to see old friends who lived here.

One weekend, Margaret, our mutual friends Jean Russell and Gary Lundell, and I drove to Port Angeles and up into the Olympic Mountains to see the view from Hurricane Ridge. We stopped for lunch at the small town of Chimacum near Port Townsend. The previous evening, *The Wizard of Oz* had been on local television. Both the waitress and the cook kept staring at Margaret, thinking that she looked somehow familiar. Finally, the waitress said, "Excuse me, but has anyone ever told you that you look like that actor Margaret Hamilton?"

Margaret laughed, "Yes, I have heard that before."

"Have you ever *met* her?" the waitress asked.

"Yes, I have," Margaret answered, winking at Gary and me. "And, quite frankly, dear, I was not particularly impressed by her!"

Margaret was on vacation that day and wanted to be just one more face in the crowd. The next time I visited that cafe, I did tell the waitress that she had indeed waited on Margaret Hamilton. I gave the waitress and the cook personal greetings from Margaret.

JEAN RUSSELL had an apartment on Queen Anne Hill, overlooking Elliott Bay and the Seattle skyline. She was a very good cook. Margaret and I often spent the evening at Jean's apartment while Margaret told us countless stories about her film-making life and especially about the complications of filming *The Wizard of Oz*. "We never dreamed that *The Wizard of Oz* would be such a success — and would continue to be so popular," she added.

WHEN MARGARET WAS BACK in New York I often phoned her to report some of the news of our mutual friends. In 1981 I mentioned to her that Katharine Hepburn had recently been to Seattle, performing in a play. Miss Hepburn had spent two afternoons visiting the Burke Museum, where I had just met her.

"I was in a film with Miss Hepburn once," Margaret exclaimed. "It was *State of the Union*, with Spencer Tracy. I had only a small part, but Miss Hepburn was so kind to me. The director wasn't satisfied with the way I spoke my few lines, or with the camera angle. He was impatient. He wanted to move along to the next scene. Miss Hepburn stopped him, and told him firmly: 'This is Margaret's best moment in this film. We're not going to go on until it's just right.' Can you imagine, so famous a star as Katharine Hepburn being that thoughtful toward a minor performer such as me?"

Margaret seemed entirely accessible and outgoing. She was infinitely attentive and devoted to her friends. She personally answered every fan letter sent to her and every request for an autograph. "This is my responsibility. If children and fans take the trouble to write me, I certainly should make every effort to respond," she explained. Jean Russell, Gary Lundell and I sat for several evenings at Jean's dining room table while Margaret inscribed dozens and dozens of photographs, adding a personal message to each admirer and autograph collector.

Margaret was never a theatrical prima donna. Her kindnesses were expressed simply and without any to do. When she returned to New York, or when she was traveling, she remembered our birthdays with presents and cards, even a phone call. When she went to India to visit her family who were briefly there, she visited a dealer of rare East Indian gems and minerals. Knowing I liked and collected minerals and fossils, she mailed me a package of rare, beautiful zeolite crystals. I later donated these delicate crystal clusters to the Burke Museum collection.

During her last visit to Seattle, Margaret, Jean Russell, young student Cory Taylor, and I had spent the afternoon visiting painter Guy Anderson and his friend Deryl Walls in La Conner. Guy took us to lunch at his favorite restaurant, the Lighthouse. We visited sculptor Phil McCracken and his wife, Anne, on Guemes Island. Later that day, driving toward Jean's beach cabin on Guemes Island, Margaret turned to me from the front seat, saying firmly and mischievously, "Dear,

I don't have much time left. I'm eighty now, you know. I've courted you quite long enough. I want you to be my husband!"

Not hesitating for an instant, I exclaimed, "Oh, Maggie, I accept!"

Margaret stared at me in the back seat "You do?" she asked nervously.

"Of course, I do. It isn't as if we haven't known each other very long."

"Oh, oh," murmured Margaret to herself, apprehensively.

When Jean dropped me off in the University District and I got out of the car, Margaret kissed me gently on the cheek. "Do be careful now, dear. It's taken me such a long time to find you, and I don't want to lose you. Please do take good care of yourself!" she said.

Several months later, I phoned her in New York. "Do you remember our conversation in Seattle?" I asked.

Cautiously, she answered, "Yes, I do. What about it?"

"But, Maggie — don't you think it's a good idea?"

"Yes, I like the idea of it well enough, just as long as we keep it just an idea. *If* you know what I mean!"

Thus, I found myself somewhat abstractly betrothed to Margaret Hamilton.

MARGARET'S MEMORY BEGAN TO FAIL HER. She was no longer able to perform on the stage, or even to do bit parts for television. She was no longer able to live alone in her Gramercy Park apartment. Her family arranged for her to be near them in a Connecticut nursing home, where they could visit her regularly. After a performance at Lincoln Center, as we walked down the street together, Margaret had once turned to me and said, "When I die, I want it to be on stage. Just after I've given the performance of my life!" This was a wish that would not come true for her.

I phoned her at the nursing home. We had a brief conversation, mostly about her visit to Seattle. Would I please remember her to Jean and Gary, she added. A few days later she died. I had sent her a postcard from Boulder, Colorado. The card was on the table next to her bed, her family told me.

The word of her death spread quickly around the world. A mythic American icon had died, a living and enduring part of the childhood of so many of us. Several days later, her family sent me a clipping from the *Baltimore Sun*. It was a cartoon, without any caption. There, in the sky, on her broomstick, was the Wicked Witch of the West, Maggie, flying straight toward the Pearly Gates of Heaven. They were all festooned with garlands, lit up, awaiting her.

Biographical
Notes

LÉONIE ADAMS

b. December 9, 1899, Brooklyn, New York
d. June 27, 1988, New Milford, Connecticut
One of the most esteemed lyric poets of her generation, Adams made her reputation during the 1920s and 1930s for poetry marked by "striking metaphor, a deeply mystical view of nature, vigorous metrics, and by a sense of song that lends delicacy to the packed meaning of her lines" (W. R. Benét). T. S. Eliot considered her a master of the sonnet form, and poet Allen Tate said of her poems: "More than anyone else, she continues at the highest level the great lyrical tradition of the English Romantics, with whom in their own time she would have held her own." Today her books are hard to find except in Rare Book Rooms and in some university libraries.

After graduating from Barnard College in 1922, she edited *The Measure*, a literary magazine, and published her first volume of poetry, *Those Not Elect*, in 1925, followed by *High Falcon and Other Poems* in 1929. In 1933, she edited (as translator, with others) *The Lyrics of Francois Villon*. Her last book, *Poems: A Selection*, won the Bollingen Prize for Poetry in 1955. She taught the writing of poetry in New York City, as a Fulbright lecturer in France, and as a visiting professor at the University of Washington and at Purdue. She served as Consultant in Poetry to the Library of Congress (1948–49). Adams's numerous honors and awards include the National Institute of Arts and Letters Grant in Literature (1949), the Shelley Memorial Award (1954), the Academy of American Poets Fellowship (1959), and the National Council of Arts Grant (1966–67).

GUY ANDERSON

b. November 20, 1906, Edmonds, Washington
d. April 30, 1998, La Conner, Washington
Although Guy Anderson received national attention in 1953, when *Life* magazine touted him as one of four "Mystic Painters of the Northwest," he would be characterized in 1977 by Adelyn Breeskin, curator of art at the National Collection of Fine Arts, Smithsonian Institution, as "one of the least well known of our important American painters." For most of his life he lived in Washington state, keeping a low profile and painting in relative seclusion in La Conner, a fishing village north of Seattle.

In 1929 painter Morris Graves, then age nineteen, sought

out Anderson after seeing his work exhibited in Seattle. During the decade that followed, they traveled and lived together, visiting Mexico and California and sharing studio space and ideas. Graves introduced Anderson to Asian art and philosophies, and Anderson acquainted Graves with Western art history. During the 1920s Anderson studied painting in Seattle with well-known artist Eustace Paul Ziegler. From 1933 to 1944 he was on the staff of the Seattle Art Museum. In 1936 he had his first solo exhibition at the Seattle Art Museum, and in 1952 he had a solo show at the Zoe Dusanne Gallery in Seattle. He toured Greece, Italy, and France in 1967, and again in 1975 as the recipient of a Guggenheim fellowship.

During the 1970s and 1980s he painted many of his most compelling and original works. In 1974 the National Collection of Fine Arts (now called the National Museum of American Art) at the Smithsonian Institution mounted an exhibition featuring works by Anderson, Graves, Tobey, and other Northwest artists. A major retrospective in 1977 was organized jointly by the Seattle Art Museum and the Henry Art Gallery at the University of Washington, and in 1982 his work was exhibited at the National Museum of Art in Osaka, Japan. His works are represented in New York in the collections of the Metropolitan Museum of Art and the Brooklyn Museum, and in Washington, D.C., in the Phillips Collection, as well as in museums in Dublin, Rotterdam, Santa Barbara and Stanford (California), Portland (Oregon), and Seattle. For his ninetieth birthday, the Seattle Art Museum assembled a retrospective of his major works, and KCTS (Seattle) and National Educational Television produced a television documentary on his life and work.

ELIZABETH BISHOP

b. February 8, 1911, Worcester, Massachusetts
d. October 6, 1979, Boston, Massachusetts

As an undergraduate at Vassar College in the early 1930s (A.B., 1934), Elizabeth Bishop first majored in music composition and piano, but she changed her major to English Literature and began to publish her poems while she was still a college student. Poets Robert Lowell, Marianne Moore, and Randall Jarrell soon recognized the distinctive originality of her superbly crafted, witty poetry, remarkable for its descriptive power, and they praised her work in the influential literary journals of the era. She was welcomed as a poet's poet, and publication of her first book of poems, *North & South*, in 1946 contributed to her growing reputation. She was awarded a Guggenheim Fellowship in 1947, the first of numerous honors, and she held the Poetry Consultancy at the Library of Congress during 1949–50. In 1952 she settled in Brazil, where she would live until 1966 and where she began writing some of her finest poems. In 1955, she reprinted her first book, with additions, as *Poems: North & South — Cold Spring*. It was awarded a Pulitzer Prize.

In 1966 Bishop came to Seattle to teach poetry at the University of Washington. This marked the beginning of her role as both poet and teacher. She taught at New York University, M.I.T., and Harvard University, where, in July 1973, she accepted a four-year appointment as lecturer in poetry. Earlier that year she had returned to Seattle to teach a course in the English department and to give a poetry reading in the Theodore Roethke Memorial Series. Among her most noted former students are Pacific Northwest poets Sandra McPherson, Henry Carlile, and Duane Niatum.

Bishop's books of poetry include *Questions of Travel* (1965), *The Ballad of the Burglar of Babylon* (1968), *Geography III* (1976), and *The Complete Poems, 1927–1979* (1983). Her prose works include *The Diary of "Helena Morley"* (translation, 1957), the text of the Time-Life World Library book on *Brazil* (1962), *The Collected Prose* (1984), and *One Art* (letters, 1994).

ERNEST BLOCH

b. July 24, 1880, Geneva, Switzerland
d. July 15, 1959, Portland, Oregon
Ernest Bloch's major compositions reflect Jewish themes and liturgy and show as well a strong neoclassical trend, combining musical forms from past European traditions with twentieth-century techniques. He studied with noted Swiss composer Emile Jaques-Dalcroze and in Belgium with violinist Eugene Ysaye. He taught and lectured at the Geneva Conservatory during 1911, where pianist Berthe Poncy Jacobson studied with him. Bloch first came to the United States in 1916 as conductor for Maud Allen and her dance company. Settling in New York, he composed his *Israel Symphony* (1916) and gained significant attention with the tone poem *Schelomo* (*Solomon*, 1916) for cello and orchestra. His *Suite for Viola and Piano* (1919) was awarded the Coolidge Prize and quickly earned a place in the literature. He served as

founding director of the Cleveland Institute of Music (1920–25) and was then director of the San Francisco Conservatory (1925–30). He settled in Agate Beach, Oregon, in 1941 and shortly afterwards accepted a position as professor of music composition at the University of California in Berkeley, where he taught summer courses until his retirement in 1952. In his later years, Bloch was accorded numerous honors, including the Gold Medal in Music from the American Academy of Arts and Sciences (1947), and two awards from the New York Music Critics' Circle (1952). Wary of worldly success, he confided to visitors that the agates he found on the beach near his Oregon house were of more interest and significance to him than ephemeral prizes. Many of his works, most notably his second *Concerto Grosso* (1952) and his five string quartets, occupy an important place in twentieth-century music.

IMOGEN CUNNINGHAM

b. April 12, 1883, Portland, Oregon
d. June 24, 1976, San Francisco, California
A major figure in the history of contemporary photography, best known for her photographs of plants and for her portraits, Imogen Cunningham moved to Seattle as a child in 1893, where her family settled on Queen Anne Hill. She began taking photographs in 1901 through a correspondence course. In 1907 she graduated from the University of Washington with honors in chemistry. There was no art department at that time, so there were no courses in photography, but she

studied physics, literature, German, and French. Upon graduating, she worked for two years in Edward S. Curtis's commercial photography studio in Seattle, where she learned the process of platinum printing. A Pi Beta Phi scholarship for $500 for study abroad enabled her to study photochemistry in 1909 at the Technische Hochschule in Dresden, Germany. While there, she attended the International Photographic Exposition in Dresden and familiarized herself with the best work being done in Europe and America at that time. She later opened her own successful portrait studio in Seattle, where her clientele included many prominent members of Seattle society.

In 1915 she married etcher and painter Roi Partridge, with whom she bore three sons. They moved to northern California in 1917, where Partridge ultimately chaired the art department at Mills College, Oakland. Cunningham ceased to do commercial photography until 1921. In 1929, through Edward Weston's recommendation, ten of her plant photographs were included in international exhibition of avant-garde photography in Stuttgart, Germany.

After separating from her husband in 1934, Cunningham made her home in San Francisco. In 1947 she became a visiting instructor in the photography department of the California School of Fine Arts (now the San Francisco Art Institute). The department was headed successively by photographers Ansel Adams and Minor White. Cunningham's photographic portraits from these years, including her 1950s studies of Morris Graves and Theodore Roethke, are among her most memorable works.

At the age of ninety, Cunningham embarked upon a series of portraits entitled *After Ninety*, documenting the lives of scores and nonagenarians, including her own. In 1973 Morris Graves posed again for her, in a touching portrait of the two of them together. Even during her final years, she insisted on personally printing from her own negatives and carefully controlling the quality of any work that bore her signature. The major holdings of her work are now at the Imogen Cunningham Archives of the Imogen Cunningham Trust in Berkeley, California. A significant group of her work is also in the photographic collections of the Henry Art Gallery at the University of Washington.

ZOE DUSANNE

A remarkable collector, art dealer, and early champion of major European and American artists, Zoe Dusanne played a singularly important role in the history of avant garde painting in the Pacific Northwest. She was probably born in or around 1890, but as in many other aspects of her life, she remains a mysterious, legendary presence in the Seattle art scene of the 1950s and 1960s. As Mark Tobey said of her, "There will never be anyone like Zoe again!" Before coming to Seattle, she lived in New York City, where she had sought out and befriended painters whose works she admired and collected, including such artists as Lyonel Feininger, Marcel Duchamp, and Stuart Davis.

Dusanne was not only ahead of the times in the Northwest area art scene but she often singlehandedly shaped it and gave it a highly cultivated focus. It was her calculated suggestion to a staff acquaintance at *Life* magazine that led to the seminal 1953 article on "Mystic Painters of the Northwest." This article brought national attention to the Pacific Northwest and codified the art world's perception of the cutting edge of "Northwest Art." As a dealer, she introduced works to the Seattle area by artists who, though often little known at the time, became household names in the pantheon of modern painting: Piet Mondrian, Paul Klee, Jean Arp, Matta (Roberto Echaurren), Francis Picabia, Sonia Delaunay, Robert Delaunay, Sam Francis, and others. Dr. Richard Fuller, founder and director of the Seattle Art Museum, purchased many important paintings from Dusanne's private collection, works which he then gave to the Museum. As a close friend of collector Peggy Guggenheim, Dusanne was responsible for Guggenheim's donation to the Seattle Art Museum of a major painting by Jackson Pollock. Dusanne herself donated important contemporary works to the Museum and to the Henry Art Gallery.

Her death in 1972 was a profound loss to the Seattle art scene. Several years later, the Seattle Art Museum mounted an exhibition of paintings that had either been in her private collection or had been placed by her in museum and important private collections. Of the many art dealers who have been active in the history of Northwest art, Dusanne represented an early high standard for her unflinching integrity in collecting and exhibiting only those artists in whose works she fiercely believed.

MORRIS GRAVES

b. August 28, 1910, Fox Valley, Oregon

Although Morris Graves is largely self-taught in the techniques of art, his style was greatly influenced by three trips he made to Japan before the age of twenty as a cadet on the American Mail Lines. His lifelong study of and commitment to Asian art and philosophy, especially the tenets of Zen Buddhism, are reflected most profoundly in his delicate, radiant, metaphysically charged paintings of animals and plants, which are among the most intensely private and original works of our time.

During the 1930s Graves shared a studio with painter Guy Anderson in Edmonds, Washington. In 1936 his first one-man show was presented at the Seattle Art Museum. A year or so later, he turned from oils to tempera or gouache, which he applied to Chinese mulberry paper. Many of his most famous works, including the *Inner Eye* series, the *Journey* series, and the *Joyous Young Pine* series, were painted between 1940 and 1947 at his isolated studio-home on Fidalgo Island near Anacortes, Washington. In 1947 he built another home-studio at Woodway Park, near Edmonds, and in 1964 he designed the house and studio in a redwood forest near Loleta, in northern California, where he presently lives in seclusion. He also has traveled widely, to Europe, Asia, Africa, South America, and the Near East.

In recent years Graves has continued to paint and exhibit internationally. His work, both early and recent, is well represented in major museum collections in the United States, Japan, and Europe. In the Pacific Northwest, important collections of Graves's work are owned by the Seattle Art

Museum, the Henry Art Gallery, the Museum of Northwest Art in La Conner, Washington, and the Museum of Art
at the University of Oregon in Eugene.

PEHR HALLSTEN

Born in 1897 in Hammerdal, in the Jamtland district of north-
central Sweden, Pehr (as he signed his paintings) was a
scholar, a tutor in foreign languages, and a long-time companion to Mark Tobey, from 1940 until Pehr's death in Basel,
Switzerland, in 1965. He and Tobey first met in the late 1930s
in Ballard, a Scandinavian enclave of Seattle, several years after Pehr's arrival from Sweden. During the early 1950s Pehr
felt the need to obtain further formal schooling and to acquire "academic respectability." He enrolled as a graduate
student in the department of Scandinavian languages and literature at the University of Washington, where he wrote his
thesis on Swedish playwright August Strindberg. A somewhat
whimsical man, he was proud of his belated Master of Arts
degree and enjoyed being addressed thereafter as "Professor
Hallsten."

Encouraged by Mark Tobey and Helmi Juvonen, he first
began to paint in 1953. His highly distinctive paintings, based
on his childhood memories, were instantly popular among
collectors and other artists. His exhibitions in New York and
Europe were praised by critics and museum curators, a success which both surprised and amused Pehr. He wore his erudition lightly, and his works combine a sophisticated humor
with an almost childlike delight in depicting Scandinavian

mythological creatures as well as the many colorful characters he encountered on Seattle's University Way or in its Public Market. When people suggested that his brightly colored paintings reminded them of Marc Chagall's work, Pehr would blink, look innocent, and say, "Chagall? Who is that? I've never heard of him!"

His work is well represented in Pacific Northwest museum collections, notably those of the Henry Art Gallery, the Nordic Heritage Museum (Seattle), the Seattle Art Museum, and the Art Gallery of Greater Victoria (B.C.). A large collection of Pehr Hallsten's work is in the Mark Tobey papers at the Manuscripts, Special Collections, University Archives Division, University of Washington Libraries.

MARGARET HAMILTON

b. 1902, Cleveland, Ohio
d. May 17, 1985, Salisbury, Connecticut
Margaret Hamilton dreamed as a young woman of entering the world of the theater and making her own way as a professional actor. But she was the daughter of a prominent attorney, and both of her parents insisted that she find another career, something more financially stable. She became a schoolteacher upon graduating from college and for several years taught kindergarten classes at the Rye Country Day School in New York. Luck stepped in when she helped a friend audition for a part in the 1932 Broadway play *Another Language*. Her own reading was so notable that she was hired on the spot, quite unexpectedly, for a role in what turned out to be the surprise hit of the New York season. This play was

made into a movie and became Hamilton's ticket to Hollywood, where she pursued a long and very successful career,
appearing in character roles in more than seventy films, including *The Wizard of Oz* (1939), *My Little Chickadee* (1940)
with Mae West and W. C. Fields, *State of the Union* (1948)
with Katharine Hepburn and Spencer Tracy, and *Brewster
McCloud* (1970). She never lost her love of the stage, and
whenever she could, she interrupted her film career to take
roles in repertory and regional theater. She also had running
parts in several television series, including *The Egg and I* and
Ethel and Albert, and in two soap operas. She appeared in television commercials throughout the 1970s as "Cora," the
New England storekeeper who sells only Maxwell House coffee. During the 1970s she also performed in several plays with
the Seattle Repertory Theater, perhaps most memorably as
"Mrs. Malaprop" in Sheridan's comedy *The Rivals*. In her
later years she made her home in New York, but she had
so thoroughly enjoyed the Pacific Northwest and the new
friends she met there that she continued with great delight to
revisit Seattle.

BERTHE PONCY JACOBSON

b. 1894, Geneva, Switzerland
d. October 2, 1975, Seattle, Washington
A prominent figure in Seattle's musical community for nearly
fifty years, Berthe Poncy Jacobson received her early musical
training at the Geneva Conservatory of Music, where she
studied under composer Ernest Bloch. In his later years,
Bloch characterized her as having been "my best student of

all!" Her teachers at the conservatory also included Swiss composer Frank Martin. She was awarded a scholarship to the Schola Cantorum in Paris, where she studied composition with Vincent d'Indy, founder and director of the Schola Cantorum, and piano with Blanche Selva and Alfred Cortot. She received two diplomas from this institution, one in musical composition, one in piano. She later studied piano at the Geneva Conservatory with Bernhard Stavenhagen, who had been Franz Liszt's student.

Upon coming to America, she joined the faculty of the Cornish School of Allied Arts in Seattle in 1924, later becoming head of the piano department there. She married pianist-composer Myron Jacobson, a fellow teacher at the Cornish Institute, with whom she performed two-piano recitals throughout the Pacific Northwest. Mrs. Jacobson joined the University of Washington music faculty in 1937. She retired in 1965, but continued to teach and coach. Her students included pianist-composer Lockrem Johnson, pianist Myung Whun Chung, and pianist-composer William Bolcom, winner of the 1982 Pulitzer Prize in music.

Berthe Poncy Jacobson and Mark Tobey enjoyed a close and enduring friendship that was of great importance to each. Upon Jacobson's death, Tobey sent a cablegram from Basel which read: "[I am] very much saddened by the passing away of my friend Berthe Poncy (Mrs.) Jacobson. Her talent she so unselfishly handed down until lately to younger generations. To me she gave the keys to unfathomable joys of the world of music."

HELMI JUVONEN

b. *January 17, 1903, Butte, Montana*
d. *October 18, 1985, Elma, Washington*
At the age of fifteen, Helmi Juvonen moved to Seattle with
her Finnish immigrant parents. She graduated from Queen
Anne High School and studied art during the late 1920s at the
Cornish School of Allied Arts, where she met Mark Tobey in
1929. From 1938 to 1940 she worked on the Federal Arts Project in Seattle with artists Mark Tobey, Morris Graves, Hans
Bok, Fay Chong, Jacob Elshin, and Julius Twohy. At this time
she also met Dr. Richard Fuller, founder and director of the
Seattle Art Museum, who would be her major patron for
many years. Her only other formal art training was from 1943
to 1945, when she worked for the Boeing Company and attended evening classes in mechanical drawing and general
engineering at the University of Washington. Until the mid-
1950s, she continued to sell her prints herself each Saturday
from a booth in the Seattle Public Market.

In subject matter, Juvonen's art reflects not only the cultural mythologies of her Finnish heritage but also her strong
interest in the cultures of the Native American peoples of the
Pacific Northwest. During the 1940s she attended, by invita-
tion, the Swinomish and Lummi tribal ceremonies near La
Conner and Bellingham, as well as ceremonial gatherings
of the Yakima (now Yakama) and Vancouver Island tribes,
sketching and painting what she observed. In 1951 she spent
a week at Neah Bay on Washington's Olympic peninsula,
sketching the Makah tribe's ceremonial dances.

But much of her art is uniquely her own. In the early
1950s, inspired by her obsessive but unrequited love for Mark

Tobey, Juvenon painted some of her most startling and powerful works, particularly her notorious *Helmi and Mark* series. In 1959, owing to increasing eccentricity, she was appointed a ward of the state and was sent to the Oakhurst Convalescent Center in Elma, near Olympia, Washington, where she would live out her remaining years. After many years of relative obscurity as an artist, her final decade (1975– 85) witnessed six retrospective exhibitions of her paintings at museums in Seattle, Olympia, and Bellingham. Her highly original contributions, both to regional art and ethnology, have led to her growing recognition as a significant figure in the cultural history of the Pacific Northwest. Following her death, a memorial exhibition was organized in 1986 by the Cheney Cowles Museum in Spokane, which owns a large collection of her works. Her works are also in the collections of the Henry Art Gallery, the Seattle Art Museum, the Museum of Northwest Art (La Conner), the Whatcom Museum of History and Art (Bellingham), and the Nordic Heritage Museum (Seattle). Helmi Juvonen's correspondence and sketch books are in the Manuscripts, Special Collections, University Archives Division, University of Washington Libraries.

SUSANNE K. LANGER

b. December 20, 1895, New York, New York
d. July 17, 1985, Old Lyme, Connecticut
As one of the first women in the United States to become a professional philosopher, Susanne Langer was an intellectual and cultural pioneer who wrote extensively on aesthetics and the philosophy of science. She drove herself rather rigorously,

realizing that she had to be twice as good a philosopher as her male counterparts in order to be taken seriously, let alone accepted professionally by them. As a child on the Upper West Side of Manhattan, she was ill for several years and gained most of her early schooling at home with tutors. Her father, a New York lawyer, played the piano and cello, and she also learned to play both instruments. Her musical proficiency gave her a practical expertise on which to base her later studies of the philosophy of music and afforded her an uncommon advantage over many theoretical philosophers. Her father did not believe in college education for women; her mother thought otherwise. After her father died, her mother sent her to Radcliffe College. She graduated in 1920 and obtained her Ph.D. in philosophy from Harvard University in 1926.

At Radcliffe, Langer studied with Alfred North Whitehead, who later wrote the foreword to her first book, *The Practice of Philosophy* (1930). In her book *Philosophy in a New Key: A Study in the Symbolism of Reason, Rite, and Art* (1942), she sought to give art the claim to meaning that science was given through Whitehead's analysis of symbolic modes. In *Feeling and Form* (1953), she distinguished the nondiscursive symbols of art from the discursive symbols of scientific language and suggested that art, especially music, is a highly articulated mode of expression symbolizing intuitive knowledge that cannot be conveyed by ordinary language.

From 1954 to 1962, Langer was professor of philosophy at Connecticut College in New London. During the academic year 1952–53, she was visiting professor in philosophy at the University of Washington. She was an exacting and highly demanding teacher, and few of her students managed to complete their studies with her. During her stay in Seattle, she studied cello privately with faculty cellist Eva Heinitz, and she became good friends with painter Guy Anderson. On a later visit to Seattle in 1966, she met poet Elizabeth Bishop; they shared an admiration for each other's work.

During her emeritus years, Langer gave full attention to her last book, a three-volume study entitled *Mind: An Essay on Human Feeling* (1967, 1972, and 1982), in which she sought to trace the origin and development of the mind. In 1986, this study was singled out by the editors of Johns Hopkins University Press as being the one book in their century-long publishing history that "by its content has made the greatest mark in the world of culture and ideas." During her lifetime, the originality and importance of Langer's philosophical contributions were appreciated by noted physicists Robert Oppenheimer and Niels Bohr, and she is increasingly regarded as one of the major philosophers of the twentieth century.

THEODORE ROETHKE

b. 1908, Saginaw, Michigan
d. 1963, Bainbridge Island, Washington
Theodore Roethke graduated from the University of Michigan and later took courses at Harvard University. He taught English literature and creative writing at Lafayette College, at Pennsylvania State University, and at Bennington College before moving permanently to the University of Washington in 1948, where he was poet-in-residence. Roethke's first book of poems, *Open House* (1941) demonstrated his mastery of the

short lyric form, and with the publication of his book *The Lost Son* in 1948, his work began to occupy an important place in modern American poetry. With publication of *The Waking* (1953), which was awarded a Pulitzer Prize, *Selected Poems* (1958), and *The Far Field* (1964), Roethke joined the ranks of the major American poets of his time. In 1963 he died of a heart attack while swimming. His students included such notable poets as James Wright, Richard Hugo, Carolyn Kizer, and David Wagoner. The Theodore Roethke Papers are in the Manuscripts, Special Collections, University Archives Division, University of Washington Libraries.

RICHARD SELIG

b. October 29, 1929, New York, New York
d. October 14, 1957, New York, New York
A young poet of exceptional talent, Richard Selig was the son of a Wall Street corporation lawyer. He grew up on Long Island. In his teens, his family moved to Washington, D.C. After high school, he began to travel, studying psychology at Occidental College in Los Angeles and then, on a scholarship, studying painting at the Museum of Modern Art in New York. He spent a year in France, studying French at the Sorbonne. He arrived in Seattle in October 1950, having come to study verse writing with Theodore Roethke. While in Seattle, he formed several important friendships, including one with Mark Tobey. His first poems were published here in 1954 in Carol Ely Harper's magazine, *Experiment,* in an issue guest-edited by Richard Eberhart.

Awarded a Rhodes Scholarship in 1953, he studied next at Oxford University. His tutor during his first year at Magdalen College was C. S. Lewis, author of *The Screwtape Letters*. While at Oxford, Selig was diagnosed by a close friend, a medical student, as having a virulent form of leukemia, and he was given at best only a few more years to live. The medical student was the now-famed neurologist and writer Oliver Sacks. After Selig's marriage to Irish singer Mary O'Hara in 1955, they lived first in London and then settled in New York, where he worked as a public relations writer with the Western Electric Company until his death in 1957.

During his lifetime, his poetry was championed by poet Stephen Spender and was published in several prominent English literary journals, including *Encounter* and *The Listener*, and in the international journal *Botteghe Oscure* in Rome. Among his many posthumous tributes was an eloquent appreciation of his talents written by Theodore Roethke and published in *Encounter*. A small volume of his collected poems, edited by Peter Levi, was published by Dolmen Press in Ireland in 1962. Richard Selig's student notebooks from his work with Roethke during 1950–52 are with the Theodore Roethke Papers, Manuscripts, Special Collections, University Archives Division, University of Washington Libraries.

MARK TOBEY

b. December 11, 1890, Centerville, Wisconsin
d. April 24, 1976, Basel, Switzerland
Mark Tobey spent his childhood years in Tennessee, Wisconsin, and Indiana. In 1908 his father sent him to Saturday

classes at the Art Institute in Chicago. He soon found employment locally as a commercial artist. Working as a fashion artist and doing numerous charcoal portraits, he was given his first exhibition of portrait drawings at the M. Knoedler Galleries in New York in 1917. The following year he became a member of the Baha'i World Faith, the beginning of a lifelong interest in non-Western philosophy and religion.

In 1923, after an unsuccessful marriage, he moved to Seattle and taught at the Cornish School of Allied Arts. That same year he met Teng Kwei, a Chinese student at the University of Washington, who introduced Tobey to Chinese calligraphy. In 1934, Tobey spent one month in a Kyoto monastery, where, contrary to Pacific Northwest folklore, he did not "achieve enlightenment." Instead, he studied calligraphy and wrote poetry. His development in 1934 of a style that would later be known as "white writing" marked an important contribution to twentieth-century abstract painting. Art historian Elizabeth Bailey Willis showed painter Jackson Pollock some of Tobey's early white writing works at the Willard Gallery in New York while she worked there during the 1940s. Pollock's "overall" technique, it can be documented, had some of its roots in Tobey's early experiments in white writing. In 1958 Tobey was awarded first prize in painting at the XXIX Biennial in Venice. Several years later, in 1961, he was invited to have a major exhibition at the Musee des Arts Decoratifs (Palais du Louvre) in Paris, followed by a retrospective at the Museum of Modern Art in 1961.

From 1923 until 1960, when he settled permanently in Basel, Switzerland, Tobey lived mostly in the University District in Seattle, traveling frequently during the spring and summer, and usually spending the winter in Seattle, painting, practicing the piano, composing music, and, all in all, living a relatively uneventful but productive life while sharing a house with his companion, painter Pehr Hallsten. He died in Basel in 1976 and is buried there along with Pehr and with Tobey's close friend and secretary, Mark Ritter. A major retrospective of his paintings and drawings, with an accompanying catalog illustrating over 300 of his works, was held at the Museo Nacional Centro de Arte Reina Sofia in Madrid in 1997–98.

Although Tobey spent much of his life living far removed from the "cutting edge" of contemporary art movements, he is nonetheless often identified with the pioneering origins of twentieth-century abstract painting. He did, however, once remark to his painter friend Guy Anderson, while they were discussing modern painting after Cézanne, "Who knows, it may turn out that all of us painters have been barking up the wrong trees!" Tobey's work is well represented in the collections of the Seattle Art Museum and the Henry Art Gallery. An extensive collection of his personal papers is in the Manuscripts, Special Collections, University Archives Division, University of Washington Libraries. Other of his papers are at the Archives of American Art, Smithsonian Institution, Washington, D.C.

Index of Names